Christine Möhle

Trials and Tragedies

Phil Ochs and his Rehearsals for Retirement

Mit Beiträgen von:

Christine Möhle
Kasper Nijsen
Huw Spink

2017

Trials and Tragedies: Phil Ochs and his Rehearsals
for Retirement / Christine Möhle

Umschlag: Phil Ochs, Juni 1968, Burg Waldeck Festival
unter Verwendung eines Fotos von Lothar Schiffler

Fotos: Lothar Schiffler, München und Jay Cassidy,
University of Michigan Library Digital Collections / Michigan Daily
Alumni Photographers
Zeichnungen: Lindsay Mercer
Illustrationen/Faksimiles: Burg Waldeck Archiv, bearbeitet von Winfried Arndt
Übersetzung aus dem Deutschen: Maria Diaz-Pinés und Doris Harries
Übersetzung aus dem Dänischen: Xenia Wieth

© 2017 Christine Möhle,
für namentlich gezeichnete Beiträge bei den Autoren

Herstellung und Verlag
Tredition GmbH, Hamburg

ISBN: 978-3-7439-3963-9 (Paperback)
ISBN: 978-3-7439-3964-6 (Hardcover)
ISBN: 978-3-7439-3965-3 (e-Book)

Das Werk, einschließlich seiner Teile, ist urheberrechtlich geschützt. Jede Verwertung ist ohne Zustimmung des Verlages und des Autors unzulässig. Dies gilt insbesondere für die elektronische oder sonstige Vervielfältigung, Übersetzung, Verbreitung und öffentliche Zugänglichmachung.

Bibliografische Information der Deutschen Nationalbibliothek:
Die Deutsche Nationalbibliothek verzeichnet diese Publikation in der Deutschen Nationalbibliografie; detaillierte bibliografische Daten sind im Internet über http://dnb.d-nb.de abrufbar.

*My responsibilities are done let them come let them come
and I realize these last days these trials and tragedies
were after all only
our rehearsals for retirement.*

(Phil Ochs)

Für Markus und Tobias

Inhalt / Contents

Vorwort und Danksagung / Foreword and
Acknowledgements   7

The revolution catches up with the revolution of the
songmakers – Phil Ochs auf dem Burg Waldeck Festival
/ Phil Ochs at the Burg Waldeck Festival
von / by Christine Möhle
Übersetzung / Translation: Maria Diaz-Pinés   12

The times have radicalism in the air
Gespräch mit Phil Ochs / Interview with Phil Ochs
Übersetzung / Translation: Doris Harries   62

Demonstrations are more important than you think –
so keep on / Demonstrationere betyder mere end I tror
– så I må blive ved
Übersetzung / Translation: Xenia Wieth   83

Konzerte in Europa 1968 / Concerts in Europe 1968   91

William Butler Yeats visits Lincoln Park
by Christine Möhle   92

Where were you in Chicago	97
Phil Ochs in Chicago	103
Chronology of Events	108
Phil Ochs: Rehearsals for Retirement by Kasper Nijsen	114
Farewell to the Muse: Phil Ochs' Rehearsals for Retirement by Huw Spink	117
Literaturhinweise / Bibliographical References	129
Bildnachweis / Picture credits	130

Vorwort und Danksagung

1968 war ein bewegtes Jahr. Für Phil Ochs war es ein entscheidendes, geprägt durch eine Vielzahl von Unternehmungen. Bereits 1967 hatte er zwei Demonstrationen gegen den Krieg in Vietnam organisiert und er setzte seine künstlerischen und politischen Aktivitäten im Jahr 1968 fort. Er war beteiligt an der Gründung der Yippies und sang für Senator Eugene McCarthy in dessen Wahlkampf. Zudem veröffentlichte er im Sommer ein neues Album, *Tape from California,* trat in unzähligen Konzerten auf und startete eine Tour durch Deutschland und Skandinavien im Juni. Im August war er einer der wenigen Künstler, der die Proteste während des Parteitages der Demokraten in Chicago unterstützte. Das Ergebnis des Parteitages, auf dem Vizepräsident Hubert Humphrey zum Präsidentschaftskandidaten der Demokraten nominiert wurde, wie auch die exzessive Polizeigewalt während des Parteitages, ließen Phil Ochs desillusioniert und deprimiert zurück. Hatte er vor Chicago noch von einer Hoffnung der Verzweiflung gesprochen, dass das politische System in den USA fähig zur Reform sei, hatte diese Hoffnung sich für ihn weitgehend zerschmettert, wozu die Nominierung Richard Nixons auf Seiten der Republikaner sicherlich beitrug. Dennoch – oder vielleicht besser – trotzdem, veröffentlichte er im folgenden Jahr sein zornigstes, traurigstes und, ja auch zärtlichstes, Album – *Rehearsals for Retirement.*

Dieses Buch versucht einige von Phil Ochs' Aktivitäten während dieses Jahres näher zu beleuchten: seine Auftritte auf dem Burg Waldeck Festival, seine Tour in Skandinavien und Deutschland, die Ereignisse in Chicago und sein Album *Rehearsals for Retirement*.

Ich möchte allen danken, die mir bei diesem Buch in vielfältiger Weise geholfen haben. Mein Dank gilt vor allem Peer Krolle, Leiter des Waldeck-Archivs, für seine großzügige Unterstützung und für seine mit mir geteilten Erinnerungen an Phil Ochs. Ihm und Jürgen Behling vielen Dank für einen inspirierenden Tag auf der Waldeck.

Ferner möchte ich Lothar Schiffler und der Michigan University Library danken für die Copyright-Erlaubnis der Fotos. Mein Dank gilt außerdem Winfried Arndt für viele hilfreiche Gespräche und seine Unterstützung bei der Aufbereitung alter Zeitungsartikel und Fotos.

Nicht zuletzt möchte ich Maria Diaz-Pinés, Doris Harries und Xenia Wieth für ihre Übersetzungen danken. Ohne Marias Hilfe hätte ich es außerdem nie geschafft, aus einer Vielzahl von Dateien ein Buch zu gestalten. Danke Lindsay Mercer für deine Zeichnungen von Phil. Mein Dank gilt natürlich besonders Kasper Nijsen und Huw Spink für ihre Beiträge. Huw hat darüber hinaus viele Artikel gegengelesen und wertvolle Tipps gegeben.

Und vor allem gilt mein Dank meinem Mann und meinem Sohn, die geduldig dieses Projekt begleitet haben.

Foreword and Acknowledgements

1968 was an eventful year. For Phil Ochs it was crucial and marked by a variety of activities. As early as 1967 he had organized two demonstrations against the war in Vietnam and he continued his artistic and political activities in 1968. He was involved in the founding of the Yippies and sang for Senator Eugene McCarthy in his election campaign. He also released a new album in the summer, *Tape from California*, performed in countless concerts and started a tour of Germany and Scandinavia in June. In August, he was one of the few artists who supported the protests during the Democratic National Convention in Chicago. The result of the Convention, with its nomination of Vice President Hubert Humphrey as Democratic candidate for the presidential election, as well as the excessive police force during the Convention, left Phil Ochs disillusioned and depressed. If before Chicago he had still spoken of a *hope of despair* that the political system in the US was capable of reform, largely this hope of his was shattered, in part certainly due to the Republican's nomination of Richard Nixon. Still – or perhaps more accurately – in spite of, he was able to release his angriest, saddest and indeed also his most tender album – *Rehearsals for Retirement*.

This book attempts to shed some light on several of Phil Ochs' activities during this year: his performances at the Burg Waldeck Festival, his tour of Scandinavia and Germany, the events in Chicago and his album *Rehearsals for Retirement*.

I would like to thank all those who in many different ways helped me with this book. My thanks go to Peer Krolle, director of the Waldeck Archive, for his generous support and for sharing his memories of Phil Ochs with me. Thanks to him and Jürgen Behling for an inspiring day on the Waldeck.

I would also like to thank Lothar Schiffler and the Michigan University Library for copyright permission of the photos. My thanks also go to Winfried Arndt for many helpful conversations and his assistance with the preparation and processing of old newspaper articles and photos.

Last but not least, I would like to thank Maria Diaz-Pinés, Doris Harries and Xenia Wieth for their translations. Maria also helped me create and design a book from a variety of files. Thank you Lindsay Mercer for your drawings of Phil. My special thanks, of course, go to Kasper Nijsen and Huw Spink for their contributions. In addition Huw also checked through many articles and gave valuable tips.

And above all, I wish to thank my husband and my son, who patiently accompanied this project.

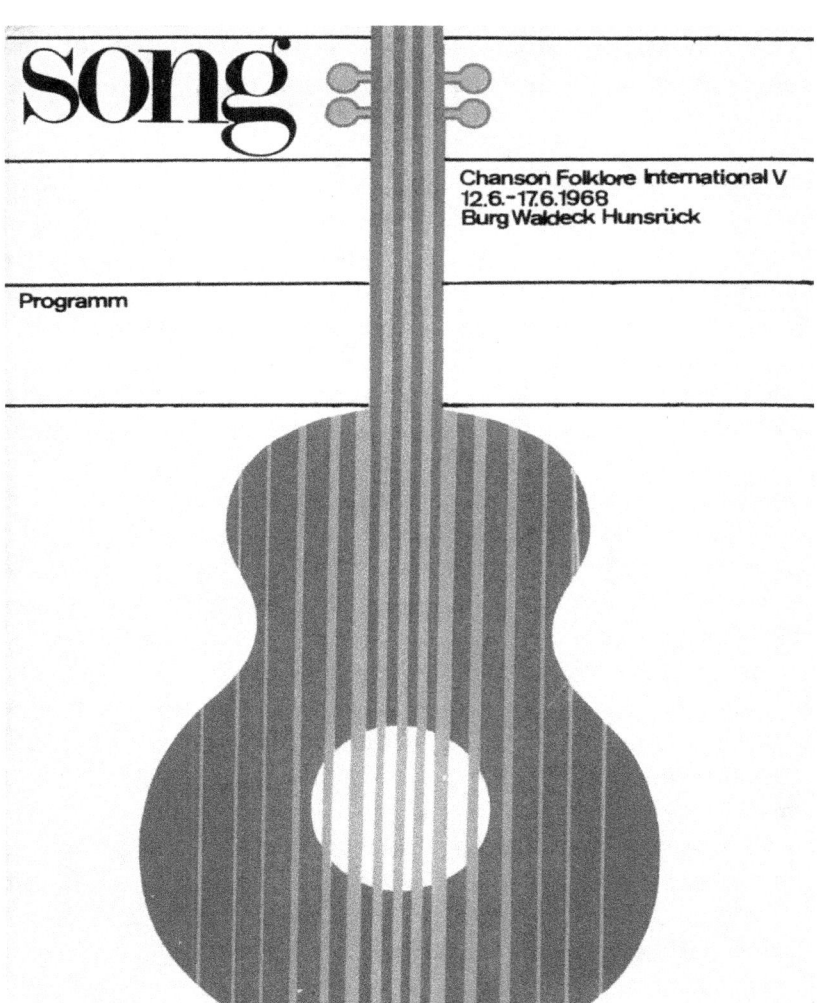

"The Revolution catches up with the revolution of the songmakers" – Phil Ochs auf dem Burg Waldeck Festival

Als Phil Ochs Anfang Juni 1968 die USA für eine Konzertreise in Europa verließ, ließ er ein Land hinter sich zurück, von dem er Monate später in einem Interview sagte: "I was in Los Angeles when Kennedy was shot and the next day was on a plane for Copenhagen for a series of concerts in Europe. I thought America had gone mad." [1]
An dem Tag, an dem Senator Robert F. Kennedy, jüngerer Bruder John F. Kennedys und vielversprechender Präsidentschaftskandidat der Demokraten, seinen Verletzungen erlag, stand Phil Ochs bereits auf einer Bühne in Lund, Schweden.
Vielleicht erinnerte ihn dieses Konzert an einen Auftritt zwei Monate zuvor in Chicago, als er am Tag nach der Ermordung Martin Luther Kings in der dortigen Orchestra Hall ein Konzert gab, "ill, but on with show" [2] und am Ende seines Auftrittes *Crucifixion* sang, sein Lied über die Massen, die ihre Helden erst verehren, um sie dann zu ermorden und später zu einem Mythos zu verklären.
Auf jeden Fall sang er es eine Woche später bei seinen Auftritten während des Burg Waldeck Festivals und höchstwahrscheinlich auch während seines Auftrittes an der Universität von Lund.
Um in die kleine, beschauliche Universitätsstadt im Süden Schwedens zu gelangen, hatte Ochs einen Direktflug von Los Angeles nach Kopenhagen nehmen müssen, und von dort aus ein kleineres Flugzeug nach Malmö in Schweden. Die Strecke von Malmö nach Lund beträgt dann nur noch gut 20 km. Phil reiste, zumindest anfangs, in Begleitung seines Bruders und Managers, Michael Ochs. [3] Im Gepäck hatte er die brandneue Pressung seines gerade fertiggestellten fünften Albums *Tape from California*. [4]
Phils Auftritt an der Universität von Lund war der erste einer kleinen Tournee, die ihn außer nach Schweden noch in die norwegischen und dänischen Hauptstädte Oslo und Kopenhagen sowie in mehrere deutsche Städte führen sollte.

Vermutlich war diese Tour für Phil Ochs eine willkommene Gelegenheit, seinem „verrückt gewordenen" Land für eine Weile den Rücken zu kehren. Er hatte in verschiedenen Interviews in den letzten Monaten wiederholt verkündet, dass er über Auswanderung nachdächte. Auch in seinen Interviews in Schweden und Dänemark sprach er von der Möglichkeit einer Auswanderung nach Kanada oder ein Land "somewhere in Europe" [5] und sah explizit diese Tournee als eine Möglichkeit, neue Eindrücke zu gewinnen "and get a feel of how America looks from over there. And then I'll make a decision one way or the other." [6]

Gleichzeitig sah er natürlich die Möglichkeit, seine neuen Lieder einem interessierten Publikum in Europa vorzustellen. [7]

Ochs Auftritte in Skandinavien fanden ein positives Echo in der dortigen Presse, die über ihn und seine Konzerte in mehreren Artikeln berichtete. [8] In einem Interview, das mit ihm während des Festivals auf der Waldeck geführt wurde, äußerte er sich erfreut über den positiven Verlauf seiner Europa-Reise und über die Möglichkeit, im schwedischen Fernsehen aufzutreten, etwas, das ihm „in den USA verwehrt" werde. Ihn begeisterte die noch überall greifbare revolutionäre Stimmung, die er in den USA zunehmend vermisste und die ihn an die Zeit der Bürgerrechtsbewegung 1963 erinnerte. [9]

Nach einem letzten Konzert in Schweden reiste Phil Ochs weiter zum Burg Waldeck Festival in den Hunsrück.

Man kann nur erahnen, was er von der idyllischen Abgeschiedenheit gehalten und wie er überhaupt dorthin gefunden hat – empfohlen worden war ihm jedenfalls von Rolf Gekeler ein Flug nach Frankfurt. Aber im Grunde verwundert es kaum, dass Phil gerade an diesem Festival teilnahm, das das politischste in der Geschichte der Waldeck Festivals werden sollte, trotz des reichlich belanglosen Mottos „Lied 68". Es war ein hochpolitisches Jahr, auch in Deutschland, und es erscheint fast logisch, dass Phil Ochs mit dabei war.

Die Burg Waldeck Festivals haben ihren Namen von einer mitten im Hunsrück, idyllisch im Baybachtal gelegenen Ruine: der Waldeck. Ihre abgeschiedene Lage – die nächste größere Stadt, Koblenz, ist immerhin rund 45 km entfernt – prädestiniert sie nicht unbedingt für die Abhaltung von Musikveranstaltungen. Und dennoch fanden hier in den 1960er Jahren sechs Festivals statt, die der Waldeck den Ruf eines deutschen Newports eintrugen.

Trägerverein und Ausrichter der Festivals war die *Arbeitsgemeinschaft Burg Waldeck* (ABW), die aus dem linksliberalen Flügel des *Nerother Wandervogels* und Akteuren verschiedener deutscher Jungenschaften entstanden war. Dem bunten Treiben auf der Waldeck misstrauisch bis feindselig gegenüber stand der konservativ-autoritär ausgerichtete Flügel der *Nerother*. [10]

Der *Nerother Wandervogel* [11] – unter der Führung der Zwillinge Robert und Karl Oelbermann – hatte 1920 die Burgruine für sich entdeckt. Im Laufe der Jahre wurde Land aufgekauft und bewirtschaftet, erste Hütten gebaut, Fahrten auch in ferne Länder unternommen und ganz allgemein dem Ideal einer gesunden, heimatverbundenen und zukunftsfrohen Jugend gehuldigt. Die Struktur der *Nerother* war dabei streng hierarchisch und wenn Robert Oelbermann von der Burg als „... Quell reinen, kraftvollen jugendlichen Lebens..." [12] sprach, kann „Jugend" getrost durch „junge Männer" ersetzt werden, Frauen wurden bereits Anfang der 20er Jahre aus dem *Nerother Wandervogel* ausgeschlossen.

1933, nach der Machtergreifung der Nationalsozialisten, wurde der *Nerother Wandervogel* verboten, ihre Mitglieder verfolgt, die Burg überfallen und beschlagnahmt. Ein Nachfolgeverein, nun unter dem Namen *Arbeitsgemeinschaft Burg Waldeck* (ABW), musste sich 1935 auf Druck der Nazis ebenfalls auflösen, wurde aber nach dem Krieg wieder ins Leben gerufen. Er setzte sich zusammen aus ehemaligen Mitgliedern des *Nerother Wandervogels*, dem sich in den 50er Jahren diverse jungenschaftliche Gruppierungen anschlossen. Karl Oelbermann – sein Bruder Robert war 1941 im KZ Dachau ums

Leben gekommen – in den ersten Jahren noch Vorsitzender der ABW, brach bald schon mit ihr und gründete Anfang der 50er Jahre den *Nerother Wandervogel* neu. Zu unterschiedlich waren wohl die jeweiligen ideologischen, politisch-kulturellen Ansichten. [13]
Oelbermann stritt fortan um den alleinigen Besitzanspruch an Burg und Ländereien und verlangte, auch gerichtlich, eine zwangsweise Auflösung der ABW. Erst 1978 konnte der Rechtsstreit endgültig zugunsten der *Arbeitsgemeinschaft Burg Waldeck* entschieden werden. Diese Streitigkeiten sollten auch Auswirkungen auf die Festivals haben, denn einige Mitglieder der *Nerother* scheuten später auch vor Sabotageakten nicht zurück.

Die Vorbereitungen für das erste Waldeck Festival begannen bereits 1963.[14] Die Initiative ging dabei von einem Studentischen Arbeitskreis innerhalb der ABW aus, der allerdings der Zustimmung des Ältestenrates der ABW bedurfte und auch fand. Den harten Kern innerhalb dieses Arbeitskreises bildeten Diethart Kerbs, Peter Rohland, Jürgen Kahle und Rolf Gekeler. Die interne Aufgabenverteilung sah vor, dass Peter Rohland die Kontakte zu Künstlern herstellen und ein Programm entwickeln sollte. Rolf Gekeler war für die Pressearbeit und die Betreuung der auftretenden Künstler zuständig, Diethart Kerbs sollte die Pressetexte ausarbeiten sowie den ideologischen und politischen Rahmen setzen. Für die technische und organisatorische Durchführung war Jürgen Kahle zuständig. [15]
Alle diese Arbeiten wurden ehrenamtlich geleistet und auch den Künstlern, die man einlud wurde zwar Kost und Logis zugesagt, aber keinerlei Gage gezahlt, ein Konzept, das übrigens bis zum letzten Festival 1969 beibehalten wurde.
Die ersten drei Festivals standen unter dem Motto „Chanson Folklore International". Wenn das erste, für Pfingsten 1964 geplante Festival auch noch mit dem Zusatz „Junge Europäer singen" versehen wurde, spiegelt der Titel doch ausgezeichnet die Traditionen wieder, auf die sich die Initiatoren mit ihrem Festival

beriefen. Man wollte fast vergessenes deutschsprachiges, demokratisches und sozialrevolutionäres Liedgut wiederbeleben, aber auch jiddische Folklore, französische Chansons und Strömungen britischer, aber vor allem auch US-Amerikanischer Folk-und Protestsongs aufgreifen und einem interessierten Publikum vorstellen. Eingeladen werden sollten Gruppen und Sänger aus Europa – wobei hier ausdrücklich auch der sogenannte Ostblock mit einbezogen wurde –, Israel und den USA. Inspirierend und begeisternd wirkten dabei die Ereignisse und Entwicklungen in den USA, vor allem das Festival in Newport 1963 sowie das von Berkeley ausgehende Free Speech Movement. [16]

Nach einer Planungszeit von fast einem Jahr fand das erste Festival schließlich an Pfingsten 1964, zwischen Freitag, den 15. und Donnerstag, den 21. Mai statt.
Die Anzahl der auftretenden Künstler war überschaubar und auch der Besucherandrang hielt sich mit rund 400 Gästen noch in Grenzen. [17] Das war von den Organisatoren durchaus gewollt, man wollte Raum geben für Diskussionen und Erfahrungsaustausch und war keinesfalls interessiert an einem Musik nur wie eine beliebige Ware konsumierenden Publikum. [18] Zugleich wurde auch jetzt schon, wie Diethart Kerbs in seinem Grußwort deutlich machte, Wert darauf gelegt, „... die Waldeck zu dem zu machen, was sie schon immer war: zu einem Ort der größtmöglichsten Freiheit für den Andersdenkenden. [...] Hier wollen wir [...] offene Résistance für die Toleranz üben!" [19]
Bereits beim ersten Festival mit dabei waren deutsche Künstler wie Dieter Süverkrüp und die damals noch fast gänzlich unbekannten Liedermacher Franz-Josef Degenhardt und Reinhard Mey, die auf der Waldeck ihre ersten Erfolge mit ihren selbstkomponierten Liedern feierten. Hinzu kamen Musiker wie Peter Rohland, Hein und Oss Kröher, Colin Wilkie & Shirley Hart und John Pearse, die das Programm mit jiddischen Liedern, französischen Chansons, Vagantenliedern sowie britischen und amerikanischen Folksongs bereicherten.

Verschiedene deutsche Sender waren mit Übertragungswagen vor Ort und berichteten im Radio, und auch in den Printmedien fand das Festival, wenn auch in offensichtlich geringerem Maße, seinen Widerhall.
Auch das teilnehmende Publikum war durchaus im Sinne der Veranstalter: es waren überwiegend junge Leute unter 30, viele davon Studenten, aber auch aus der bündischen Jugend stammende Teilnehmer waren gekommen. Finanziell konnte sogar – vor allem dank der ehrenamtlich geleisteten Arbeit – ein kleiner Gewinn verbucht werden. [20]

Zum zweiten Festival 1965, das in diesem Jahr von Pfingsten weg auf den Zeitraum von Mittwoch, den 26. Mai bis Dienstag, den 1. Juni verlegt worden war, kamen bereits mehr als 1000 Besucher, die optimistischste Schätzung spricht sogar von annähernd 2000. [21]
Dieses Mal waren nicht nur Rundfunksender mit ihren Übertragungswagen, sondern auch Fernsehsender mit dabei, und auch die Presse berichtete überregional. Trotz ihrer abgelegenen Lage lag das Gelände der Waldeck in der Einflugschneise der US-Amerikanischen Luftwaffe, ein Umstand, der Aufnahmen und Sendungen der Fernsehanstalten empfindlich störte. Aufnahmen mit Künstlern wurden z.T. vom Gelände der Waldeck wegverlegt, um ungestörte Übertragungen zu garantieren und von Seiten der Organisatoren wurden im Laufe der Zeit verschiedene Versuche unternommen, ungestörten Musikgenuss und Mitschnitte der Konzerte zu ermöglichen. [22]
Neben vielen Sängern, die bereits beim ersten Waldeck Festival dabei waren, kamen dieses Jahr einige neue hinzu, u.a. der zu diesem Zeitpunkt noch unbekannte Walter Mossmann, der sich hier wie viele andere, vor allem deutsche Liedermacher, einen Namen machen sollte.
Die Stimmung muss, dem schlechten Wetter zum Trotz, bestens gewesen sein, es gab neben verschiedenen Konzerten wieder Workshops und Diskussionen [23] und an einem Tag veranstalteten

die anwesenden britischen Künstler ein *Hootenanny*, als befänden sie sich plötzlich im Greenwich Village des Jahres 1963. [24]
Bereits zu diesem frühen Zeitpunkt scheint die Infrastruktur der Waldeck und der angrenzenden Dörfer an manche Grenzen gestoßen zu sein. Lebensmittel waren zumindest im kleinen Dorfladen ausverkauft, dafür scheint aber die Verpflegung auf dem Gelände der Waldeck funktioniert zu haben. Die Rede ist zumindest von Eintöpfen, Cevapcici und Kebab sowie jeder Menge Wein und Bier. [25]
Der Erfolg dieses zweiten Festivals führte dazu, dass der Kreis der Organisatoren für das nächste Festival deutlich erweitert wurde. [26]

Das dritte Festival 1966 war in 3 Etappen über elf Tage hinweg geplant. Von Donnerstag, den 26. bis Samstag, den 28. Mai fanden als „Arbeitstreffen" deklarierte Zusammenkünfte statt, an denen gemeinsam musiziert, zugehört und diskutiert werden sollte. Die hauptsächlichen Musikveranstaltungen waren für das Pfingstwochenende vom 28. – 30. Mai vorgesehen. Für die Zeit vom 31.5. bis zum 5.6. schloss sich eine „Folksong-Woche" an, die hauptsächlich aus Workshops bestand, die sich so breiten Themen wie altdeutschen Lautenliedern, elisabethanischen Sonetten, französischen Chansons und amerikanischen Bluestechniken widmete. [27]
Zum dritten Waldeck Festival kamen bereits an die 3000 Besucher. [28] Die Veranstalter hatten mit der Einbeziehung der Medien, sowie dem Aufbau einer eigenen Zeitschrift – der von Rolf Gekeler herausgegebenen Zeitschrift *Song* –, bewusst auf eine breitere Öffentlichkeit gezielt. Auf der anderen Seite machte sich aber auch zunehmend das Gefühl breit, an die Grenzen des Möglichen zu stoßen.
Die Infrastruktur auf der Waldeck war nie für breite Massen angelegt, wenn auch in diesem Jahr erstmals das Rote Kreuz die Versorgung der Festivalteilnehmer übernahm, und auch versucht worden war, die sanitäre Situation durch den Bau neuer Latrinen

besser in den Griff zu bekommen. Unabhängig von diesen infrastrukturellen Problemen ging mit der zunehmenden Bekanntheit des Festivals und der damit verbundenen Zunahme an Zuschauern oder auch bloß Neugierigen, die das Pfingstwochenende zu einem Ausflug zur Waldeck nutzten, die durchaus gewünschte Intimität ein Stück weit verloren.
Man wollte einerseits ein überschaubares, das Miteinander und den Diskurs pflegendes Festival mit Workshops, Diskussionen und spontanen Musikdarbietungen, sah sich andererseits aber konfrontiert mit dem Zustrom immer breiterer Massen, die weniger am Diskurs und mehr am Konsum der dargebotenen Musik interessiert waren.
Die Fernsehsender machten „sich … breit", das wiederholte Proben für die Live-Ausstrahlungen wurde als „bleierne Künstlichkeit" wahrgenommen [29], die man hinnahm, weil mit den eingenommenen Tantiemen für die Übertragungsrechte ein Großteil des Festivals finanziert wurde. Auch der Steigerung der Bekanntheit der auftretenden Sänger und Sängerinnen kamen die Fernsehaufnahmen durchaus zugute.
Zu diesem Festival hatten sich an die 50 Künstler eingefunden. Neben den bereits zuvor eingeladenen Liedermachern wie Walter Mossmann, Reinhard Mey und Franz-Josef Degenhardt, waren diesmal zum ersten Mal Hanns Dieter Hüsch und Hannes Wader dabei. Colin Wilkie & Shirley Hart, Hein und Oss Kröher und John Pearse waren wieder gekommen, aus den USA war Hedy West mit dabei und aus Israel Aviva Semandar. Für Hannes Wader, der, wie er berichtete, mit klammen Fingern und verstimmter Gitarre nervös drei Lieder sang, war es der Durchbruch. [30]

Peter Rohland, Mitorganisator der Festivals und dort auftretender Künstler, konnte in diesem Jahr nicht mehr teilnehmen. Er war im April völlig überraschend mit nur 33 Jahren an einer Gehirnblutung gestorben. [31]

Die zunehmende Popularität der Waldeck Festivals hatte sicherlich auch mit dem zunehmenden „Folkboom" in Westdeutschland zu tun. Mit fast dreijähriger Verspätung war das Interesse an politisch relevanten Liedern auch in der Bundesrepublik Deutschland angekommen. [32]

Das vierte Festival 1967, das unter dem Motto „Das engagierte Lied" stand, fand in der Woche von Mittwoch, den 24. bis Sonntag, den 28. Mai statt. Nach der Erfahrung mit dem letztjährigen Festival wollte man bewusst die Zuschauerzahlen reduzieren, indem man den Termin von Pfingsten wegverlegte und zudem mit Voranmeldungen für das Festival arbeitete.

Es gibt keine genauen Angaben über die Zuschauerzahlen, nach einem zeitgenössischen Bericht sollen es 2–3000 Zuhörer gewesen sein, wobei auch dort schon festgestellt wurde, dass eine genaue Schätzung nahezu unmöglich sei. [33] Auf jeden Fall aber scheint das Ziel der Veranstalter, die Zuschauerzahlen zu reduzieren, erreicht worden zu sein.

Im Mittelpunkt des Festivals sollte das gesellschaftskritische, engagierte politische Lied stehen, worunter man in erster Linie politische Chansons, deutschsprachige Gegenwartslieder und sozialkritische Folk-und Protestsongs verstand. Der immer populärer werdenden Beatmusik standen große Teile des Organisationsteams eher skeptisch gegenüber, da man ihr, im Gegensatz zur politischen Folkmusik und zur Protestmusik, nicht zutraute, zur politischen Willensbildung und einem gesellschaftskritischen Bewusstsein beizutragen.

Ganz unwidersprochen blieb dieser Ansatz allerdings nicht, es gab durchaus Stimmen, die dieses Konzept rückwärtsgewandt fanden und auf mehr Pop und Underground Musik setzen wollten. Es ging dabei auch darum, ob diese Musik eine politische Bedeutung hatte und wie weit eine gewisse Kommerzialisierung zugelassen werden sollte. Wollte man im „Ghetto" der Waldeck bleiben oder einen eher urbanen Rahmen wählen für künftige Veranstaltungen?

Die Mehrheit des Organisationsteams wandte sich aber weiterhin gegen eine Kommerzialisierung des Protestsongs – und auch wenn man sich bewusst war, das gerade über Senderechte ein Großteil des Festivals finanziert werden musste – sollte das *neue Lied* nicht dazu dienen, Geschäfte zu machen. [34]

Zur Waldeck gekommen waren auch in diesem Jahr wieder Walter Mossmann, Franz-Josef Degenhardt, Reinhard Mey und Hannes Wader. Hanns Dieter Hüsch trat auf, Schobert & Black, Kristin Bauer-Horn und das Schnuckenack Reinhardt Ensemble mit „Zigeunerjazz". Hedy West war da, auch Colin Wilkie & Shirley Hart und aus Spanien die Katalanen Joan & José sowie Francesc Pi de la Serra. Eine offizielle Kulturdelegation aus der DDR war ebenfalls angereist, deren „verstaubter Vortrag" voller „Revolutions-Romantik" aber eher für allgemeine Heiterkeit auf Seiten der Zuhörer sorgte. [35]

Zum ersten Mal wurde über das Festival auch international berichtet, so in der US-amerikanischen Musikzeitschrift *Sing Out*, Radio Televisione Italiana brachte einen 45minütigen Bericht und es gab wieder Beiträge sowohl im deutschen Fernsehen wie auch im Radio. [36]

Überschattet wurde das 1967er Festival von Sabotageakten, die wohl von Seiten des *Nerother Wandervogels* ausgingen. So wurden u.a. Autoreifen zerstochen, Starkstromleitungen und Mikrofonkabel zerschnitten und Trinkwasserbehälter entleert. Nach Beendigung des Festivals wurde dann auch noch die hölzerne Freilichtbühne in die Luft gesprengt. [37]

Wenige Tage nach Beendigung des vierten Festivals wurde am 2. Juni 1967 bei einer Demonstration anlässlich des Schah-Besuches in Berlin der Student Benno Ohnesorg von einem Polizisten erschossen. Nicht erst seitdem gärte es in der Republik, die vornehmlich studentischen Proteste richteten sich u.a. gegen den Krieg in Vietnam, aber auch gegen die als Aushöhlung der Demokratie empfundenen Notstandsgesetze.

Am 9. Oktober 1967 wurde in Bolivien Ernesto Che Guevara ermordet, neben Ho Chi Minh eine der Ikonen der Protestbewegung.

Am 4. April 1968 wurde der Führer der Bürgerrechtsbewegung Martin Luther King in den USA erschossen, wenige Tage später in Westberlin ein Attentat auf Rudi Dutschke verübt, das dieser schwer verletzt überlebte. Daraufhin kam es in Westberlin und mehreren anderen deutschen Städten zu Protesten und Unruhen, die als *Osterunruhen* in die Geschichte eingingen.

In der CSSR war mit dem Prager Frühling die zarte Hoffnung aufgekeimt, dass eine politische Reform innerhalb des real existierenden Sozialismus möglich sei. In Frankreich erschütterten Generalstreik, Straßenschlachten und Barrikadenkämpfe im Mai die Republik.

In den USA wurde Robert F. Kennedy ermordet, nur eine Woche vor dem für Mitte Juni angesetzten Festival auf der Waldeck. [38]

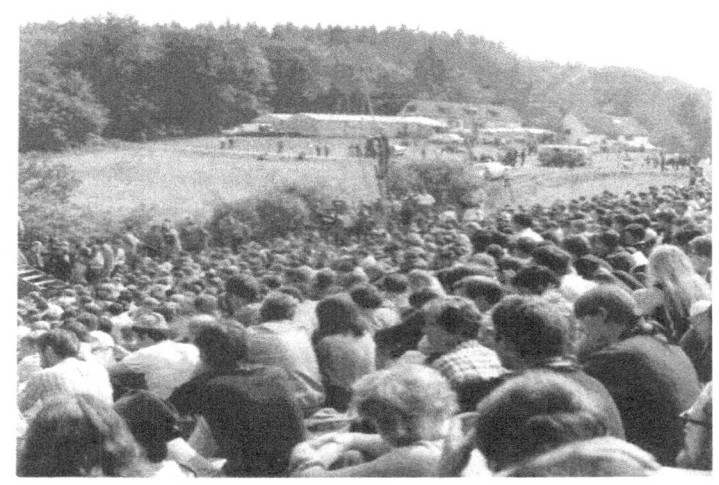

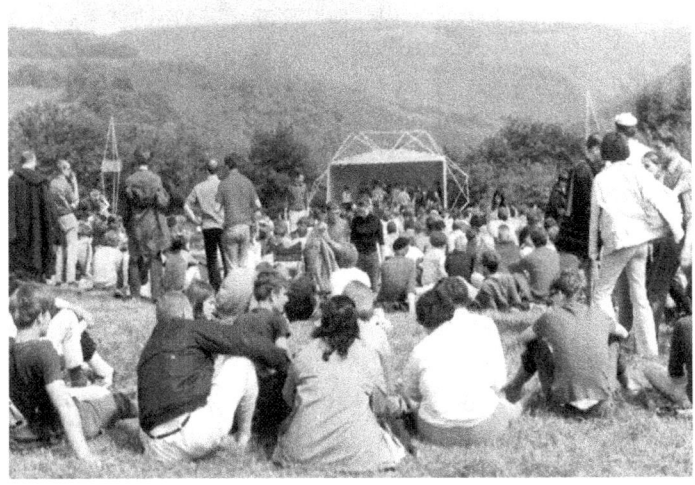

Burg Waldeck Festival Juni 1968

"The times have radicalism in the air" – Das fünfte Waldeck Festival 1968

Das fünfte Festival fand von Mittwoch, den 12.6. bis Montag, den 17.6. unter dem reichlich unverfänglichen Motto „Lied 68" statt. Die Zuschauerzahlen sprengten jeglichen Rahmen, an die 5000 sollen es gewesen sein, zeitgenössische Quellen gehen allerdings von weniger aus und sprechen von etwa 3000 Besuchern. [39]
Eingeladen waren wieder um die 50 Künstler, neben altbewährten „Veteranen" wie Fanz-Josef Degenhardt, Hanns Dieter Hüsch, Walter Mossmann, Reinhard Mey, John Pearse, Colin Wilkie & Shirley Hart waren dieses Mal auch mehrere Künstler aus den USA dabei. Neben kritischen deutschen Liedern, Chansons und Kabarett sollte in diesem Jahr „... der amerikanische Protestsong im Mittelpunkt des vorgesehenen Programms" stehen. [40]
Rolf Gekeler, der künstlerische Leiter des Festivals, hatte bereits im Sommer 1967 das Newport Folk Festival in den USA besucht und während dieser Reise offensichtlich Phil Ochs, Odetta und Guy Carawan für das Waldeck Festival im nächsten Jahr verpflichtet. [41]
Auf jeden Fall konnte Rolf Gekeler in einem Schreiben an den Bayerischen Rundfunk vom Februar 1968 damit werben, dass „... heute schon Phil Ochs sein Kommen zugesagt" habe. [42]

In einem Bericht, den Rolf Gekeler in der deutschen Zeitschrift *Song* veröffentlichte, [43] äußerte er sich verwundert darüber, dass „... jene herausragenden Stimmen der jüngeren Generation, die in Newport vor Jahren ihre ersten großen Erfolge feierten und durch die das Festival in Newport seinen legendären Ruf als 'Mekka des Folksong' bekommen hat" nicht mehr anzutreffen sind. [44] Und stellte fest: „Die Wortführer der 'Protest-Generation' singen nicht mehr in Newport."
Gekeler konstatierte, durchaus kritisch, weiter: „Die jungen Liedermacher sind in eine Art innere Emigration gegangen. [...] Die Sehnsucht nach Geborgenheit und Liebe ist ihnen im Augenblick

wichtiger als alle politischen Fragen. [...] An die Stelle von Argumenten und Diskussionen, an die Stelle des zeitkritischen Protestes, setzt die jüngere Sängergeneration Amerikas das Gefühl, das Glück und als Symbol weltumfassender Liebe, die Blume."

Gekelers Kritik verwundert wenig, wenn man bedenkt, dass Newport immer auch Vorbild und Inspiration für die Waldeck Festivals war. Auch war die Ausrichtung der Waldeck Festivals weiterhin weit entfernt von den unpolitischen „...Pseudokulturen der blumenschwenkenden Hippies" wie Gekeler etwas süffisant anmerkte.

Der Rückzug aus der Politik, der in den USA bereits eingesetzt hatte und den Phil Ochs in den folgenden Jahren so vehement beklagen sollte, hatte in der Bundesrepublik Deutschland zu diesem Zeitpunkt noch nicht begonnen. Die Atmosphäre war angespannt und die politischen Ereignisse sollten auch an der Waldeck nicht spurlos vorbeigehen.

Nicht nur die Ausrichtung der Waldeck Festivals, die sich in ihrer ganzen Geschichte immer auch als Forum für undogmatisch-politische Diskussionen verstanden hatten, wurden in diesem Jahr ganz offen von linken Gruppen in Frage gestellt, sondern auch der Sinn von Musik und Musikern als Katalysator und Träger politischer Aktionen.

Eine *Basisgruppe Waldeck-Festival*, die sich hauptsächlich aus studentischen Gruppen verschiedener Universitätsstädte rekrutierte, stellte in einem während des Festivals veröffentlichten und verlesenen Aufruf fest, dass das Waldeck Festival keine politische Bedeutung mehr und „sich zu einer Tagung für singende Fachidioten entwickelt" habe. Weiter hieß es: „Sänger werden bei revolutionären Aktionen nicht mehr benötigt. Bei Sit-in, Go-in, Teach-in wird heute sinnvollerweise nicht gesungen sondern diskutiert in der Absicht der konkreten Aktion. [...] Wenn das Festival noch einen ernsthaft-politischen Sinn haben soll, sind statt der Großkonzerte Teach-ins über die konkreten Probleme der antiautoritären Bewegung zu veranstalten. Also: Stellt die Gitarren in die Ecke und diskutiert!" [45]

Aufgerufen wurde in diesem Flugblatt zugleich zu einem Go-in bei dem am Samstag, den 15. Juni abends stattfindenden Degenhardt-Konzert. An diesem Abend sollte neben Walter Mossmann auch Phil Ochs auftreten.
Am Tag zuvor war es bereits zu Störaktionen gekommen, u.a. während der Auftritte des Liedermachers Reinhard Mey und des Sängers und Kabarettisten Hanns Dieter Hüsch. Hüsch schilderte Jahre später die Ereignisse als „...kleiner literarischer Schauprozess. Und diese rüde Menge von Chaoten glaubte, unbedingt die Kulturrevolution ausrufen zu müssen [...] und alle scheißliberalen Künstler haben zunächst einmal die Schnauze zu halten, und gesungen wird erst, wenn vorher genügend diskutiert worden ist." [46]

Laut einem Bericht der schwedischen Zeitung *Svenska Dagbladet* war Phil Ochs – zusammen mit seinem Bruder Michael – direkt nach einem Auftritt am 12. Juni in Göteborg zum Waldeck Festival gekommen. [47] Zu dem Zeitpunkt war es noch so kalt, dass Colin Wilkie, besser auf das Wetter im Hunsrück vorbereitet, den an kalifornische Temperaturen gewöhnten Ochs-Brüdern einige seiner zusätzlichen Pullover ausleihen musste. [48]
Vorgesehen war Phils Teilnahme an einem Instrumental-Workshop, der am Donnerstag, den 13.6. vormittags stattfinden sollte. Schon am nächsten Tag stand er auf der Bühne für einen Auftritt um 4 Uhr nachmittags. Angekündigt war dieses Konzert als "Phil Ochs, Workshop: Topical Song-Writing in USA". [49]

Auch wenn die Festival-Nachrichten vom 16.6. noch verkündeten: „Waldeck im Regen [...] die Wiese schwimmt, [...], die Stimmung schwimmt [...] Festzelt: brechend voll. Regen zerklopft Gitarrenklänge ..." [50] scheint das Wetter bei Phils Auftritt gut gewesen zu sein. Er stand jedenfalls auf der Open-Air Bühne, in die Sonne blinzelnd und sang seine Lieder, ungestört von Störungen vor einem offensichtlich recht entspannten Publikum. [51] Nach einem klassischen Workshop sieht das Ganze nicht aus, aber Michael Ochs hatte bereits darauf hingewiesen, dass sein Bruder ein ganzes Konzert seiner eigenen Kompositionen bevorzuge. [52]

Zum eigentlichen Politikum wurden die für den Samstag vorgesehenen Abendkonzerte mit Phil Ochs, Walter Mossmann und Franz-Josef Degenhardt.
Laut Programm sollte Ochs um 17:30 Uhr auftreten, danach waren die Auftritte Mossmanns und Degenhardts vorgesehen. Den Abschluss sollten um 23 Uhr Insterburg & Co. bilden. [53]
Es war dieses Degenhardt-Konzert, für das die *Basisgruppe Waldeck-Festival* zu einem Go-in aufgerufen hatte, um es „in ein Teach-in umzufunktionieren", verbunden mit der Forderung an Degenhardt, zur „Stellungnahme" der zuvor formulierten Thesen.
Die Konzerte sollten im großen Zelt stattfinden und offensichtlich war der Besucherandrang enorm. In einem zeitgenössischen Bericht heißt es, „schon eine Stunde vor Beginn der abendlichen Veranstaltung war im großen Zelt kein Platz mehr zu bekommen". [54]
Dadurch und auch wegen der Diskussionsfreudigkeit des Publikums, verzögerte sich offenbar der Beginn von Phil Ochs' Konzert. In einem Zeitungsbericht werden die Abläufe und die aufgeheizte Atmosphäre geschildert: „Bevor noch Phil Ochs beginnen konnte, wurden an der Rückwand des Zeltes zwei Vietcongfahnen und eine rote Fahne angebracht. Sofort spaltete sich die Zuhörerschaft erneut in zwei Lager. Nach langem Hin und Her und einem Kampf um die Fahnen sprach dann Franz-Josef Degenhardt ein Machtwort: 'Genossen und Genossinnen. Wenn die Fahnen nicht hängenbleiben, werden wir nicht singen.' Damit war der Kampf zugunsten der Radikalen entschieden, der Abend konnte beginnen." [55]
Vorhandene Tonaufnahmen legen ebenfalls nahe, dass Ochs damit zu kämpfen hatte, mit dem Konzert überhaupt zu beginnen und zumindest anfangs herrschte eine enorme Unruhe im Publikum. Ganz offensichtlich bekam Phil aber seine Zuhörer in den Griff,

denn alle Quellen sind sich einig, dass sein Konzert – wie auch die der anderen amerikanischen Sänger – ohne Störungen verlief. [56] Sowohl Mossmann wie auch Degenhardt kürzten ihre Auftritte radikal, um dem Publikum die Gelegenheit zur Diskussion zu geben. [57] Eckhardt Holler trug die von ihm verfassten Thesen vor, die bereits zuvor im Publikum verteilt worden waren. Ganz offensichtlich wurden diese nicht nur positiv aufgenommen, so heißt es in einem zeitgenössischen Bericht, dass ein Teil des Publikums mit Buhen und gellenden Pfiffen reagiert hätte. Auch erhaltene Tonaufnahmen bezeugen eine keineswegs ungeteilte Zustimmung. [58] Auf jeden Fall wurde anschließend heftig diskutiert, bis am späten Abend die Blödeltruppe Insterburg & Co. überraschend für Heiterkeit und Entspannung sorgte.

Von den Veranstaltern nach seiner persönlichen Meinung zu den Vorfällen im Festzelt befragt, erklärte Phil, „...daß sein politisches Ich die Umfunktionierung der Veranstaltung bejahe. Sie hätte aber wesentlich geistreicher und kürzer geschehen müssen. 'The revolution catches up with the revolution of the songmakers'. Im Übrigen wolle er gerade ein Lied darüber schreiben." [59]

Es ist leicht vorstellbar, dass Phil Ochs, der aus den USA an Yippie-Taktiken gewöhnt und mit dem Konzept des Theater des Absurden vertraut war, sich mehr Witz von den deutschen Möchtegern-Revolutionären gewünscht hätte. Er selbst ging in seiner Ansage zu seinem Lied *The War is Over* darauf ein: "I believe in militancy masked with some imagination rather than straight brawn. One of the things I've been trying to do in America is to get a lot of people to declare the war over in Vietnam. Just declare it over, from the bottom up ..." [60] Bei zwei Demonstrationen, die Phil Ochs in Los Angeles und New York im Vorjahr organisiert hatte, hatten er und seine Mitdemonstranten genau dies getan, indem sie, mit Plakaten und allerlei Krachmachern bewaffnet, durch die Straßen liefen und lauthals verkündeten, der Krieg in Vietnam sei vorbei, zum Unglauben und zur freudigen Überraschung der Passanten.

Das dahinterstehende Konzept hatte Phil selbst so erklärt: "The times demand a positive approach to demonstrations, a pro-life, joyful, energised, magnificently absurd demonstration against the sucking vacuum of war. [...] It's time for aesthetic rebellion, for creative anarchy; time for the use of surreal humor to ask now what our country is doing." [61]

Walter Mossmann, der ja am gleichen Abend wie Phil aufgetreten und ein Bewunderer seiner Musik war, erinnerte sich in seinen Erinnerungen an eine kurze Begegnung, bei der sie zusammensaßen und Ochs *Crucifixion* spielte und über Robert Kennedy redete, aber eigentümlich „desinteressiert" auf ihn wirkte. [62]

Als Reaktion auf die Störungen während der vorangegangenen Konzerte, erklärten eine Reihe von Künstlern in einem von Colin Wilkie verlesenden Text, dass sie unter den gegebenen Umständen nicht auftreten würden. Nach einigem Hin und Her fanden die für den Sonntagnachmittag vorgesehenen Konzerte und Workshops dann aber doch statt. [63]

Bereits am eigentlich letzten Tag des Waldeck Festivals am Sonntag – der Montag war nur noch für ein Schlusskonzert und eine abschließende Pressekonferenz vorgesehen – setzten die Diskussionen und Reflexionen über das Festival ein. Man kam überein – zumindest im Kreis der über das Festival Diskutierenden – „daß weder reine Agit-Prop-Schulung noch reiner Kunstgenuß Sinn des Festivals in Zukunft sein kann" und empfahl eine stärkere Analyse und Diskussion des musikalisch Dargebotenen unter Einbeziehung der Künstler und des Publikums. [64]

Am Sonntagabend kam es zudem noch zu einer Abstimmung über eine Solidaritätsadresse an die streikenden französischen Studenten. Es lagen zwei Entwürfe vor, wobei sich derjenige durchsetzte, der die „primäre Funktion" des Waldeck Festivals darin sah „Teil der internationalen Widerstandszentren zu sein". [65]

Nach Abschluss des Festivals am Montag, den 17. Juni war für den Abend ein „Querschnittskonzert" einiger Waldeck-Künstler in der

Kongresshalle in Frankfurt vorgesehen. An diesem Konzert nahm auch Phil Ochs teil, weitere Musiker waren u.a. Odetta, Colin Wilkie & Shirley Hart sowie die deutsche Gruppe Floh de Cologne.

Rolf Gekeler hatte bereits Monate zuvor in der Musikzeitschrift *Song* „...alle Interessenten, die mit diesen beiden Sängern [i.e. Phil Ochs und Guy Carawan] ein Konzert veranstalten wollen, um rechtzeitige Nachricht" gebeten. „*Song* denkt vor allem an die Mithilfe von Jugendorganisationen, Gewerkschaften, Studentenvereinigungen, Folk- und Politischen Clubs." [66] Auf diesem Wege war es zu den anschließenden Folgekonzerten Phils in Deutschland gekommen, so wurde z.B. das Konzert in Mönchengladbach von dem „Waldecker" Peer Krolle organisiert. Es fand im Mathematisch-Naturwissenschaftlichen Gymnasium statt und neben Phil trat erneut Odetta auf, die allerdings zusammen mit ihrem Bassisten den Weg nicht gefunden und sich verspätet hatte, so dass Phil länger als erwartet singen musste. [67]

Ein weiteres Konzert fand an der Technischen Universität (TU) in Berlin statt, dort trat Phil am 23.6. wieder zusammen mit Odetta auf, an dem Konzert in Karlsruhe am 24.6. nahmen u.a. Guy Carawan, Colin Wilkie & Shirley Hart teil. [68]

Auf der Waldeck indessen sollte das turbulente 68er Festival ein Nachspiel haben.
Für den 30. Oktober war eine Mitgliederversammlung anberaumt. Am Vorabend hatte sich bereits der Ältestenrat zusammengesetzt und über Konsequenzen aus dem Festival beraten. Man kam dabei zu dem Ergebnis, dass „der ursprüngliche Gedanke [....] überwuchert worden [sei] von bestimmten politischen Inhalten und 'Begleiterscheinungen' voll Intoleranz, die zu unqualifizierten Diskussionen geführt haben, die Steuerung des Ablaufs sei dabei den Veranstaltern aus der Hand geglitten. Nicht mehr das Lied, vielmehr der 'Wirbel' habe Besitz von der Sache ergriffen." [69]

Bemängelt wurden auch die hohen Ausgaben, die die Einnahmen bei weitem überstiegen hätten. Insbesondere die hohen Flugkosten für die amerikanischen Künstler wurden kritisiert. Schneider gibt an, dass das Festival einen Verlust von 4.500 DM gemacht hätte, wobei die Fahrtkosten für die amerikanischen Sänger alleine schon 20.000 DM ausgemacht hätten. [70]

Der Ältestenrat zog aus all dem das Fazit, den Gedanken an weitere Veranstaltungen nicht gänzlich aufzugeben, erklärte aber, dass „...die Veranstaltung im Jahre 1969 zunächst einmal ausgesetzt werden sollte."

In einer Stellungnahme hierzu verwiesen die Organisatoren auf den kulturellen Stellenwert, den die Waldeck Festivals mittlerweile errungen hätten und erklärten, dass Vorkommnisse wie bei dem 68er Festival in diesem Jahr „...an allen Plätzen, an denen sich geistig interessierte Jugend trifft, stattgefunden" hätten. Dennoch hätte das Festival „...ganz wesentlich im Zeichen des Liedes gestanden..." und man wäre „...mit Auswüchsen fertig geworden...". [71]

Auf der Mitgliederversammlung wurde keine endgültige Entscheidung über den Fortbestand des Festivals getroffen. Stattdessen sollte eine Arbeitsgruppe gebildet werden, die ein Konzept entwickeln sollte, wie ein künftiges Festival gestaltet werden könnte. Diese Arbeitsgruppe, die aus jüngeren „Waldeckern" bestand, legte dem Vorstand denn auch ein Konzept vor, das dieser jedoch ablehnte. Man stellte zwar fest, dass die ABW stolz darauf sein könne, die Festivals konzipiert und verwirklicht zu haben, befand aber, dass die Arbeit des Vereins sich nicht darin erschöpfen solle, alljährlich ein solches Festival zu veranstalten. Allerdings wurde ausdrücklich die Möglichkeit offengehalten, dass Gelände der Waldeck für ein Festival im nächsten Jahr zur Verfügung zu stellen, wenn andere Organisatoren einspränden. Man dachte hierbei besonders an „befreundete Jugendgruppen, denen die Sache des Festivals besonders am Herzen liegt...". [72]

Das sechste und letzte Festival fand 1969 von Mittwoch, den 10. bis Sonntag den 14. September unter dem Motto „Waldeck 69 – Gegenkultur" statt.

Erstmalig war die ABW nicht mehr Veranstalter des Festivals. Verantwortlich war stattdessen eine 18köpfige *Projektgruppe Waldeck*, zu der allerdings auch einige jüngere ABWler wie Ingo Weihe und Rolf Gekeler gehörten.

Es kamen immer noch weit mehr als 2000 Teilnehmer [73], auch wenn das Konzept vorsah, Vorträgen, Diskussionen und Workshops gegenüber der Musik einen weitaus größeren Stellenwert einzuräumen. Aber auch die dargebotene Musik hatte sich verändert. Folk, Chansons, Protestsongs spielten nur noch eine untergeordnete Rolle, einen breiteren Raum nahmen elektrisch verstärkte, sich als progressiv verstehende Bands wie Xhol Caravan, Checkpoint Charly, Amon Düül oder Tangerine Dream ein. Langjährige Waldeck-Teilnehmer wie Hannes Wader und Reinhard Mey traten zwar noch auf, aber Hüsch und Süverkrüp waren gar nicht gekommen, Degenhardt schaute nur zu einem Kurzbesuch vorbei und Mossmann hielt Workshops. Die Zersplitterung der Studentenbewegung in viele miteinander konkurrierende politische Gruppen zeigte sich auch auf der Waldeck, wie auch ein Rückzug in Drogenexperimente und eine verstärkte Innerlichkeit.

Das Fazit, das die Projektgruppe nach dem 69er Festival zog, war denn auch gemischt. Zu groß schienen die Gegensätze zwischen den verschiedenen Subkulturen. Man kam zu dem Schluss, die Debatte fortzuführen, aber nicht mehr im Rahmen der Waldeck Festivals. [74]

Größere Musikfestivals auf der Waldeck sollte es erst ab dem Sommer 1993 wieder geben. [75]

Phil Ochs letztes Konzert im Rahmen seiner Europa-Tournee war sein Auftritt in Mönchengladbach am 25. Juni. Danach reiste er zu einem privaten Aufenthalt nach England weiter, wurde dort jedoch von Beamten der Einwanderungsbehörde beinah an der Einreise gehindert. Man verdächtigte ihn ohne eine Arbeitserlaubnis in

England auftreten zu wollen. Nach einigem Hin und Her ließ man ihn schließlich einreisen. Offensichtlich plante Phil danach noch einen Besuch in Paris bevor er in die USA zurückkehrte. [76]

Auch wenn Phil Ochs nicht wieder zu Konzerten nach Deutschland zurückkehren sollte, ganz scheinen ihn die auf der Waldeck gemachten Erfahrungen nicht losgelassen zu haben. In einem Artikel, den Jerry Rubin Anfang August 1968 in der amerikanischen Untergrundzeitung *Berkeley Barb* veröffentlichte, berichtet er davon, wie er mit weiteren Yippies das Newport Folk Festival stören wollte, mit ähnlichen Taktiken wie die des deutschen SDS während eines Festivals in Deutschland. [77] Dieses von Rubin nicht näher bezeichnete Festival war natürlich das Waldeck Festival und kein anderer als Phil kann ihm davon berichtet haben.

Hier Jerry Rubins Bericht im Wortlaut: "This was all ironical because six Yippies and myself had come to Newport to disrupt the Folk Festival. We were inspired by what German SDS did to German left-wing singers at a festival last month in Germany. Midway through the concert SDS jumped on stage and took over the microphone. They called it a 'bourgeois festival' and said that people were consuming protest songs the way they consume clothes. 'The times are too revolutionary for this.' one said. After an hour of debate with the audience, they left and the concert continued amidst NLF flags and huge pictures of Ho Chi Minh. The Yippies came to Newport with similar ideas, but with no specific plan." [78]

Kurz nach seiner Rückkehr aus Chicago 1968 erwähnte Phil seine Erfahrungen in einem Interview mit Izzy Young ebenfalls. Auf die Frage, inwieweit Lieder ("writing songs") die Jugendbewegung unterstützen könnten, antwortete Phil wenig optimistisch: "I'm not sure that they can. The radical German students think that it's past that stage. The songs aren't enough obviously." [79]

Gerade als ein Sänger, der mit seinen Liedern etwas bewirken wollte, mussten die auf der Waldeck gemachten Erfahrungen, das Infragestellen der Relevanz und der Wirksamkeit politischer Lieder und ihrer Exponenten, Phil beschäftigt haben. [80]

Noch im Jahr 1971 erwähnte Phil die Ereignisse: "In 1968, when I played in Germany, I was told by the radical students that the kind of protest song I did was irrelevant to them. They were interested in action." [81]

Die Waldeck Festivals waren Geschichte, aber ein wenig scheinen die Ereignisse dort doch in Phil Ochs nachgewirkt und ihre Spuren hinterlassen zu haben.

---

1 Los Angeles Free Press, 7.2.1969, S. 5.- **2** Chicago Tribune, 7.4.1968, Section 1A, S. 12.- **3** Michael Ochs war auf der Waldeck noch mit dabei, aber nicht mehr bei Phils letztem Konzert in Mönchengladbach. Persönl. Mitteilungen von Colin Wilkie u. Peer Krolle.- **4** Sydsvenska Dagbladet Snällposten, 7.6.1968, S. 12.- **5** Politiken, 7.6.1968.- **6** Nova Vanguard, 8.5.1968, S. 15.- **7** Auf der Waldeck sang er Joe Hill, The War is Over, White Boots Marching in a Yellow Land und Floods of Florence vom Album Tape from California.- **8** So z.B. Sydsvenska Dagbladet Snällposten, 8.6.1968, S. 8; Dagens Nyheter, 10.6.1968, S. 8 u. 12.6.1968, S. 11; Information, 21.6.1968.- **9** Song, Nr.7, 1968, S. 37.- **10** Siegfried, Detlef: Time Is on My Side, S. 572.- **11** Damals noch unter dem Namen „Nerommenbund".- **12** Ausführlicher hierzu s. Schneider, Hotte: Die Waldeck, S. 51.- **13** Schneider, S. 37-52 und Reulecke, Jürgen: Von der Jungenschaft zur Studentenbewegung, S. 15-16. In: Anstöße: Diethart Kerbs als Kunstpädagoge, Fotohistoriker und Denkmalschützer.- **14** Schneider, S. 313-321.- **15** Nach Peter Rohlands Tod übernahm Rolf Gekeler dessen Aufgaben.- **16** Siegfried, Detlef, S. 571 und Schneider, S. 316-317.- **17** Lt. Reulecke (S. 19-20) waren es 13 Sänger und Sängerinnen; zu den Zuschauerzahlen s. Siegfried, S. 577.- **18** Siegfried, S. 576-577.- **19** Kleff, Michael: Die Burg Waldeck Festivals, S. 28.- **20** Siegfried, S. 576-577, Schneider, S. 328 u. Reulecke, S. 18-20.- **21** Reulecke, S. 20 u. Schneider, S. 330.- **22** Kahle, Jürgen: Von der Schwierigkeit ein Festival zu machen, S. 23. In: Kleff: Die Burg Waldeck Festivals; sowie Schreiben von Rolf Gekeler an die US-Standortkommandantur, 5.6. u. 6.6.1968, Waldeck Archiv.- **23** So soll es 14 Konzerte, 8 Theoriestunden und 8 Workshops gegeben haben, s. Schneider, S. 334.- **24** Teilnehmer dieses *Hootenanny* waren Colin Wilkie & Shirley Hart, John Pearse, Charly MacLean u. Samson Russell. Schneider, S. 336.- **25** Schneider, S. 332-334.- **26** Schneider, S. 337.- **27** Schneider, S. 342.- **28** ebd.- **29** Schneider, S. 342-343.- **30** Schneider, S. 346.- **31** Schneider, S. 340.- **32** Siegfried, S. 579-580.- **33** Hanns Dieter Hüsch in: Song, Nr. 5, 1967 u. Siegfried,

S. 584, der die Zahlen mit 1200 angibt.- **34** Siegfried, S. 583-587. Vertreter der mehr „urbanen" Richtung waren u.a. Rolf-Ulrich Kaiser, Reinhard Hippen u. Martin Degenhardt.- **35** Schneider, S. 356-357.- **36** Schneider, S. 357.- **37** ebd.- **38** s. hierzu auch: Schneider, S. 360.- **39** Schneider, S. 361 sowie verschiedene zeitgenössische Zeitungsberichte.- **40** Holler, Ekkehardt: Lied 68. In: Kleff, S. 59.- **41** ebd.- **42** Schreiben vom 5.2.1968, Waldeck-Archiv.- **43** Song Nr.5, 1967.- **44** Zu diesen Stimmen zählte er Bob Dylan, Joan Baez, Tom Paxton, Phil Ochs und Janis Ian.- **45** Festival-Nachrichten Nr.3, 16.6.1968.- **46** zitiert in: Schneider, S. 363.- **47** Svenska Dagbladet, 8.6.1968, S. 8.- **48** Persönliche Mitteilung von Colin Wilkie.- **49** Festival-Programm, undatiert, Waldeck-Archiv und Song Programmheft, 1968.- **50** Festival-Nachrichten Nr.3, 16.6.1968 S. 3.- **51** Youtube, Phil Ochs, "I Ain't Marchin' Anymore", Burg Waldeck, 1968. Zuletzt aufgerufen am 26.02.2017.- **52** Künstler-Formular für das Waldeck Festival 1968, undatiert, Waldeck-Archiv.- **53** Lied 68, Programmzettel, undatiert, Waldeck-Archiv – abweichend vom Programmheft, das Ochs' Auftritt noch für 20 Uhr ankündigte.- **54** Süddeutsche Zeitung, 18.6.1968.- **55** Badische Zeitung/Ausgabe Freiburg, 21.6.1968.- **56** Holler, S. 62 u. Schneider, S. 364.- **57** Stuttgarter Nachrichten, 24.6.1968 u. Festival-Nachrichten Nr.3, 16.6.1968 S. 4.- **58** Süddeutsche Zeitung, 18.6.1968 u. Kleff: Die Burg Waldeck Festivals, CD 10.- **59** Festival-Nachrichten Nr. 4, 17.6.1968. Offensichtlich wurde hier der dt. Begriff ‚Liedermacher' mit ‚songmaker' übersetzt, statt des korrekten engl. Begriffes ‚songwriter'.- **60** Konzert-Mitschnitt Burg Waldeck Festival.- **61** Los Angeles Free Press, 16.-22.6, 1967.- **62** Mossmann, Walter: realistisch sein: das unmögliche verlangen, S. 107.- **63** Festival-Nachrichten Nr.4, 17.6.1968. - **64** ebd.- **65** ebd.- **66** Song Nr. 6, 1968, S. 39.- **67** Sie hatten die Orte Bergisch-Gladbach und Mönchengladbach verwechselt.- Persönl. Mitteilung v. Peer Krolle.- **68** Festival-Nachrichten Nr. 3, 16.6.1968.- **69** Schneider, S. 368.- **70** ebd.- **71** Schneider, S. 369-370.- **72** ebd.- **73** Siegfried spricht sogar von 3500 Teilnehmern und bezieht sich dabei auf einen zeitgenössischen Zeitungsbericht, S. 594.- **74** Schneider, S. 373-374 u. Siegfried, S. 599-600.- **75** Schneider, S. 594 ff.- **76** Melody Maker, 27.7.1968, S. 18.- **77** Sozialistischer Deutscher Studentenbund (SDS), nicht zu verwechseln mit dem US-amerikanischen Students for a Democratic Society (SDS).- **78** Berkeley Barb, 2.-8.8.1968, S. 4.- **79** Young, Israel "Izzy": Interview on the Chicago Convention, www.marxists.org/archive/ochs/1968.- **80** Phil Ochs' Erfahrungen während der Democratic Convention waren allerdings weitaus positiver. Hier erlebte er, dass seine Musik durchaus in der Lage war, etwas zu bewirken. Wie er Izzy Young gegenüber erklärte, waren die Lieder "... an integral part of the movement while things were happening and therefore the words and the music had their greatest possible effect...."; ebd.- **81** New York Times, 11.4.1971

Quellen:

Kleff, Michael, Die Burg Waldeck Festivals 1964 – 1968 : Chanson Folklore International.- Hambergen: Bear Family, 2008 [Enthält 10 CD's mit Buch im Schuber]

Reulecke, David: Von der Jungenschaft zur Studentenbewegung : die bündische Jugend und die Festivals auf Burg Waldeck 1964 bis 1969. In: Anstöße : Diethardt Kerbs als Kunstpädagoge, Fotohistoriker und Denkmalschützer.- Essen : Klartext-Verlag, 2007

Robb, David: Protest songs in East and West Germany since the 1960s.- Rochester, New York : Camden House, 2007

Schneider, Hotte: Die Waldeck : Lieder, Fahrten, Abenteuer.- 2., überarbeitete und erweiterte Auflage. – Baunach : Sparbuchverlag, 2015

Siegfried, Detlef: Time is on my side : Konsum und Politik in der westdeutschen Jugendkultur der 60er Jahre. – Göttingen : Wallstein, 2006

Song : Chanson, Folklore, Bänkelsang. – Erlangen ; Frankfurt am Main : Gekeler ; Verlag Filmkunst, 1966-1970 [Später mit dem Zusatz: Deutsche Underground-Zeitschrift, ab 1969: Zeitschrift für progressive Subkultur]

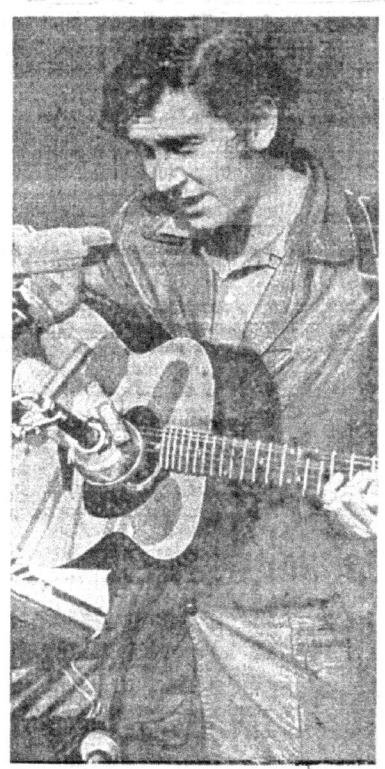
(RUNDSCHAU-Bild: Dädder)

Phil Ochs, amerikanischer Protestsänger, äußerte sich nach der Veranstaltung „Lied 68" auf Burg Waldeck zu dem Vorwurf einer kleinen Gruppe im Publikum, die engagierte Musik sei reines Konsumgut geworden: „Einst haben die Sänger die Revolution angeführt; inzwischen sind sie von ihr überholt worden." Die studentische Arbeitsgemeinschaft Burg Waldeck, Veranstalter des Chanson- und Folklore-Festivals, wollen die linken Sänger trotz der provozierten Störungen in diesem Jahr auch im kommenden Sommer wieder auf die Burg bitten.

Westfälische Rundschau, 19.6.1968

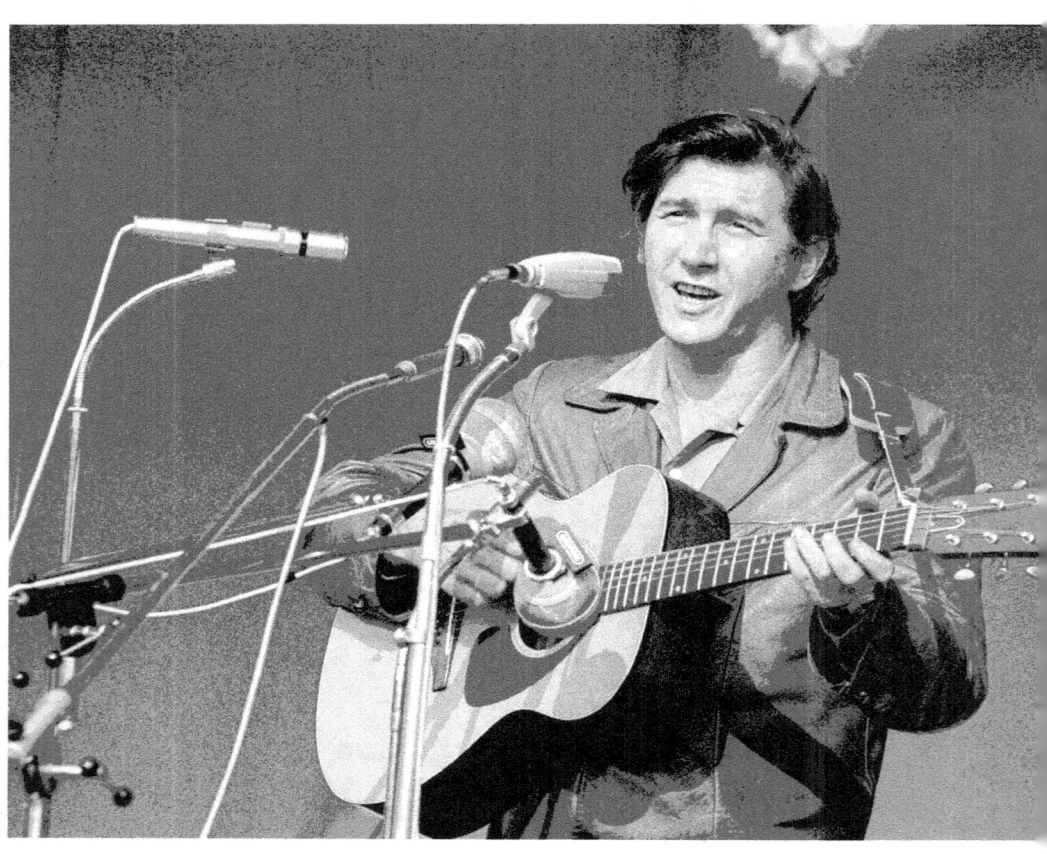

"The revolution catches up with the revolution of the songmakers" – Phil Ochs at the Burg Waldeck festival

When Phil Ochs left the United States for a concert tour in Europe in early June 1968, he left behind a country of which months later he said in an interview: "I was in Los Angeles when Kennedy was shot and the next day was on a plane for Copenhagen for a series of concerts in Europe. I thought America had gone mad." [1]
On the day when Senator Robert F. Kennedy, John F. Kennedy's younger brother and promising presidential candidate for the Democrats, succumbed to his injuries, Phil Ochs was already on stage in Lund, Sweden.
Perhaps this concert reminded him of his performance two months earlier in Chicago at Orchestra Hall, when on the day after the assassination of Martin Luther King "ill, but on with show" [2], he sang *Crucifixion*, his song about the masses that first adore their heroes, then murder them and later transfigure them into myths. In any case, he sang it a week later during his performances at the Burg Waldeck festival and most likely also during his performance at the University of Lund. To get to the small, tranquil university town in the south of Sweden, Ochs had to take a direct flight from Los Angeles to Copenhagen and from there a smaller plane to Malmö in Sweden. The route from Malmö to Lund is only 20 km. At least at first, Phil travelled accompanied by his brother and manager Michael Ochs. [3] In his luggage he had the brand new pressing of his just completed fifth album *Tape from California*. [4]
Phil's performance at the University of Lund was the first of a small tour that was to lead him to the Norwegian and Danish capital cities of Oslo and Copenhagen, as well as to several German cities.
Most likely this tour was a welcome opportunity for Phil Ochs to turn his back on his "crazy" country for a while. In recent months he had repeatedly announced in various interviews that he was considering emigration. In his interviews in Sweden and Denmark,

he spoke of the possibility of emigrating to Canada or to a country "somewhere in Europe" [5] and he explicitly saw this tour as a way to gain new impressions "and get a feel like America looks from over there. And then I'll make a decision one way or the other." [6] At the same time, he saw the possibility of presenting his new songs to an interested audience in Europe. [7]

Ochs' performances in Scandinavia met with a positive response in the local press, which reported about him and his concerts in several articles. [8] In an interview that took place during the Waldeck festival, he expressed his joy about the positive course of his European trip and the opportunity to perform on Swedish television, something that was "denied him in the USA". He was enthusiastic about the still tangible revolutionary sentiment that he increasingly missed in the United States and which reminded him of the 1963 civil rights movement. [9]

After the last concert in Sweden, Phil Ochs travelled to the Burg Waldeck festival in Hunsrück.

One can only guess what he thought of the idyllic seclusion and of how he had found his way there at all – Rolf Gekeler had recommended a flight to Frankfurt. It is, however, hardly surprising that Phil attended this particular festival, which was to become the most political in the history of the Waldeck festivals, despite its rather trivial motto "Lied 68" (Song 68). It was a highly political year, also in Germany, and thus it seems almost logical that Phil Ochs was there.

The Burg Waldeck festivals are named after the remnants of a castle in the middle of the Hunsrück region, idyllically situated in the valley of Baybach: the Waldeck. Its secluded location – after all, the nearest major city, Koblenz, is about 45 km away – does not really predestine it for the holding of music events. Nevertheless, six festivals took place there in the 1960s, which gave Waldeck the reputation of a German Newport.

The sponsoring association and organiser of the festivals was the *Arbeitsgemeinschaft Burg Waldeck* (ABW), a task force which had emerged from the left wing of the *Nerother Wandervogel* (NWV) and from various *Jungenschaften* (German youth groups). The conservative-authoritarian wing of the *Nerother* was suspicious and hostile towards the hustle and bustle taking place at the Waldeck. [10]

The *Nerother Wandervogel* [11] – under the leadership of the twin brothers Robert and Karl Oelbermann – had discovered the castle ruins in 1920. Over the years, land was bought and cultivated, the first huts were built, tours even to distant countries were made, and generally the ideal of a healthy youth, with local ties and an optimistic disposition towards the future, was embraced. The structure of the NWV was strictly hierarchical and when Robert Oelbermann spoke of the castle as a "source of pure, powerful youthful life …" [12], "youth" can easily be replaced by "young men", women had already been excluded from the *Nerother Wandervogel* since the early 1920s.

In 1933, after the seizure of power by the National Socialists, the NWV was banned, its members persecuted, the castle attacked and confiscated. It was succeeded by an association called *Arbeitsgemeinschaft Burg Waldeck* (ABW), which in 1935 also had to disband, due to the pressure of the Nazi regime, but regrouped after the war. This association was made up of former members of the NWV and was joined by various youth groups in the 1950s. Karl Oelbermann – his brother Robert had died in the Dachau concentration camp in 1941 – was ABW's chairman during the first years, but soon moved on and rebuilt the *Nerother Wandervogel* in the early 1950s. The respective ideological and political-cultural views must have been too different. [13]

Hereafter, Oelbermann contested the sole claim to possession of the castle and lands, and demanded, in court, a compulsory dissolution of the ABW. It was only in 1978 that this litigation could finally be settled in favour of the ABW. These disputes should also have an impact on the festivals, since some members of the *Nerother* did not shy away from sabotage acts.

The preparations for the first Waldeck festival began in 1963.[14] The initiative was supported by a student work group within the ABW, which, however, required the consent of the council of elders of the ABW. Diethart Kerbs, Peter Rohland, Jürgen Kahle and Rolf Gekeler formed the hard core within this work group. The internal assignment of tasks designated Peter Rohland to establish contacts with artists and to work out a program. Rolf Gekeler was responsible for the press work and the support of the artists, Diethart Kerbs was to develop the press texts as well as the ideological and political framework. Jürgen Kahle was in charge of technical and organisational implementation.[15]

All these tasks were performed on a voluntary basis, and even the artists who were invited did not receive any fees, but were promised food and lodging, a concept that was maintained until the last festival in 1969.

The first three festivals were held under the motto "Chanson Folklore International". Even though the first festival, which was planned for Whitsun in 1964, was also given the addition of "Junge Europäer singen" (Young Europeans sing), the title perfectly reflects the traditions that the initiators were referring to with their festival. On the one hand they wished to revive almost forgotten German, democratic and socialist-revolutionary songs, but also wanted to take up Yiddish folklore, French chansons and currents of British, and especially American, folk and protest songs, and introduce them to an interested audience. European groups and singers were invited, including the so-called Eastern bloc, as well as performers from Israel and the USA. The events and developments in the USA, especially the Newport Festival in 1963 as well as Berkeley's Free Speech Movement, were stimulating and inspiring.[16]

After a planning period of nearly one year, the first festival finally took place on Whitsun in 1964, between Friday the 15th and Thursday the 21st of May. The number of performers was quite manageable and with 400 guests the number of attending visitors was well within limits. [17] That was clearly the organisers' intent, since they wanted it to be a space for discussion and the exchange of experiences and were, by no means, interested in an audience consuming music just as another commodity. [18] At the same time, as Diethart Kerbs pointed out in his greeting, great importance was attached to "making the Waldeck what it had always been: a place of the greatest possible freedom for people with different opinions. [...] Here we want to practice [...] open resistance for tolerance!" [19]

Already present at the very first festival were German artists like Dieter Süverkrüp and the almost completely unknown singer-songwriters Franz-Josef Degenhardt and Reinhard Mey, who with their own song compositions celebrated their first successes at the Waldeck. In addition, musicians such as Peter Rohland, Hein and Oss Kröher, Colin Wilkie & Shirley Hart and John Pearse, enriched the program with Yiddish songs, French chansons, vagrant songs and British and American folksongs.

Various German broadcasters were on the premises reporting on the radio, and the festival was also covered by the press, albeit to a lesser extent. The attending audience was also quite in the spirit of the organisers: there were mostly young people under 30, many of them students, but also participants from *bündisch* youth groups had come. In financial terms even a small profit could be booked – mainly thanks to voluntary work. [20]

The second festival in 1965, which that year was moved from Whitsun to the period from Wednesday, the 26th of May, to Tuesday, the 1st of June, already received more than 1000 guests; the most optimistic estimate even calculated approximately 2000 visitors. [21]

This time, there were not only radio broadcasters with their mobile units present but also TV stations and the press even gave it national coverage. In spite of its remote location, the Waldeck festival grounds were situated in the approach path of the US Air Force, a circumstance which sensitively disturbed the recordings and broadcasts of the TV stations. The recording sessions with artists were partly moved away from the Waldeck area to guarantee undisturbed transmissions and the organisers even made various attempts to enable uninterrupted musical enjoyment as well as the recording of concerts without disturbances. [22]

In addition to the many singers, who were already present at the first Waldeck festival, some new ones participated this year, among them the still unknown Walter Mossmann, who like many other – especially German – songwriters was to win renown here.

Despite the bad weather, the mood must have been very good, there were workshops and discussions as well as various concerts [23], and on one of the days the participating British artists arranged a *hootenanny*, as if, all of a sudden, they were in the Greenwich Village of 1963. [24]

Already at this early stage the infrastructure of the Waldeck and the neighbouring villages seems to have reached some limitations. In the small village shop food supplies were sold out, but at least catering services on the Waldeck festival grounds seem to have been working. At any rate, sources still report of stews, cevapcici and kebab, as well as of lots of wine and beer. [25]

The success of the second festival led to a significant expansion of the circle of organisers for the next festival. [26]

The third festival in 1966 was planned to take place in 3 stages over eleven days. From Thursday, the 26th, to Saturday, the 28th of May, gatherings were held characterised as "work meetings", where people could play music together, listen to each other's opinions and take part in discussions. The main music events were scheduled for Whitsuntide, from May 28th to 30th. A "folksong week" should follow from the 31st of May to the 5th of June, consisting mainly of workshops devoted to such broad themes as old German songs for lute, Elizabethan sonnets, French chansons and American blues techniques. [27]

The third Waldeck festival was attended by almost 3000 visitors. [28]

By including the media, as well as founding their own magazine called *Song*, edited by Rolf Gekeler, the organisers had deliberately targeted a broader public. At the same time, there was also an increasing feeling of pushing the boundaries of the possible.

The infrastructure on the Waldeck was never intended for broad masses, even if that year, for the first time, the Red Cross supplied provisions for the festival's participants and attempts were made to improve the sanitary situation by building new latrines. Aside from these infrastructural problems, with the increasing popularity of the festival and consequently its rising number of spectators, further augmented by the curious, who used the Whitsun weekend for an excursion to the Waldeck, the intended intimate quality of the festival was partly lost.

On the one hand, the organisers wanted a manageable festival of workshops, discussions and spontaneous musical performances, that was meant to cultivate cooperation and discourse, but on the other, they were confronted with the influx of ever-widening masses who were less interested in participating in the discussions but rather in the consumption of the music offered.

The television stations "stretched out", the repeated rehearsals for the live broadcasts were perceived as "leaden artificiality" [29], which were accepted because for the greatest part the festival was financed by the royalties from broadcasting rights. Also the television appearances certainly benefited the rise in popularity of the performing artists.

Fifty artists came to this festival. In addition to songwriters who had previously been invited, like Walter Mossmann, Reinhard Mey and Franz-Josef Degenhardt, this time Hanns Dieter Hüsch and Hannes Wader participated for the first time. Colin Wilkie & Shirley Hart, Hein and Oss Kröher and John Pearse had come back; Hedy West was there from the USA and Aviva Semandar from Israel. It was the artistic breakthrough for Hannes Wader, who, as he later reported, nervously played three songs with clumsy fingers and an out-of-tune guitar. [30]

This time Peter Rohland, co-organizer of the festival and performing artist, was no longer able to participate. He had suddenly died of a brain haemorrhage in April, only 33 years of age. [31]

The increasing popularity of the Waldeck festivals was most certainly rooted in West Germany's rising "folk music boom". With a delay of almost three years the interest in politically relevant songs had at last arrived in the Federal Republic of Germany. [32]

The fourth festival in 1967, which had as its motto "Das engagierte Lied" (The committed song), took place in the week of Wednesday, the 24th, to Sunday, the 28th of May. After the experiences of the previous festival, the organisers consciously wanted to reduce the number of visitors by avoiding Whitsuntide and working with pre-registrations for the festival.

There is no precise information about the number of spectators, according to a contemporary report there might have been as many as 2–3000 guests, but even at the time it was established that an accurate estimation was nearly impossible. [33] In any case, the goal of the organisers to reduce audience numbers was seemingly achieved.

The focus of the festival was intended to be the socio-critical, committed political song, which primarily meant political chansons, German *Gegenwartslieder* (present-day songs) and socially critical folk and protest songs. Large parts of the organisational team were rather sceptical of the increasingly popular beat music; they didn't think that it was capable of contributing to the formation of political will and socio-critical consciousness.

This attitude, however, was not entirely undisputed. There were quite a few voices who thought the concept was retrogressive and who wanted to put on more pop and underground music. The question was whether this music had political meaning and how far commercialisation should be allowed to go. Did one want to stay in the "ghetto" of Waldeck or choose a more urban setting for future events?

The majority of the organisational team continued to oppose the commercialisation of protest songs – and, even though, they were aware that a major part of the festival had to be financed by granting broadcasting rights – the *new song* should not serve business purposes. [34]

Once more Walter Mossmann, Franz-Josef Degenhardt, Reinhard Mey and Hannes Wader came to Waldeck. Hanns Dieter Hüsch performed, as well as Schobert & Black, Kristin Bauer-Horn and the Schnuckenack Reinhardt Ensemble with "Zigeunerjazz". Hedy West was there, and so were Colin Wilkie & Shirley Hart, from Spain the Catalans Joan & José and Francesc Pi de la Serra attended. An official cultural delegation from the German Democratic Republic (GDR) also made an appearance. Their "stuffy and old-fashioned lecture" full of "revolutionary romanticism" caused general amusement in the audience. [35]

For the first time, the festival received international news coverage, such as in the US music magazine *Sing Out*, Radio Televisione Italiana broadcasted a 45 minute report and once again there were German television and radio programs. [36]

The 1967 festival was overshadowed by acts of sabotage which can almost certainly be attributed to the *Nerother Wandervogel* (NWV). Car tires were slashed, power lines and microphone cables cut and drinking water containers emptied. Also at the end of the festival the wooden open-air stage was blown up. [37]

A few days after the fourth festival ended, on the 2nd of June 1967, a police officer shot the student Benno Ohnesorg at a demonstration protesting the Shah's visit to Berlin. Even before that the atmosphere had already started to get agitated in West Germany. There were riots, mainly lead by students protesting against, amongst other things, the war in Vietnam and the *Notstandsgesetze* (German Emergency Acts), which were perceived as an erosion of democracy.

On October 9th 1967, Ernesto Che Guevara was murdered in Bolivia, next to Ho Chi Minh, one of the icons of the protest movement. On April 4th 1968, the civil rights leader Martin Luther King was shot in the USA. A few days later, in West Berlin, an assassination attempt was made on Rudi Dutschke, which he survived seriously injured. In West Berlin and several other German cities this lead to protests and riots that went down in history as *Osterunruhen* (Easter riots).

In Czechoslovakia, with the emergence of the Prague Spring movement, the delicate hope arose that political reform was possible from within the *Real Existing Socialism*. In France a general strike, street riots and barricade fights shattered the Republic in May.

In the US, Robert F. Kennedy was assassinated, just a week before the mid-June festival on the Waldeck was scheduled. [38]

"The times have radicalism in the air" – The fifth Waldeck festival 1968

The fifth festival, with the rather harmless motto "Lied 68" (Song 68), took place from Wednesday, the 12th, to Monday, the 17th of June. The attendance numbers exploded, supposedly around 5000 spectators were there; contemporary sources, however, set the number much lower and mention just about 3000 visitors. [39]

Once again around 50 artists were invited. Along well-known "veterans" such as Franz-Josef Degenhardt, Hanns Dieter Hüsch, Walter Mossmann, Reinhard Mey, John Pearse, Colin Wilkie & Shirley Hart, this time several artists from the USA were also present. In addition to critical German songs, chansons and cabaret, that year "...the American protest song was planned to be at the centre of the program". [40]

Rolf Gekeler, the artistic director of the festival, had attended the Newport Folk Festival in the USA in the summer of 1967, and while there had apparently booked Phil Ochs, Odetta and Guy Carawan for the Waldeck festival of the following year. [41]

At any rate, in a letter to the Bavarian Broadcasting Company in February of 1968, Rolf Gekeler was able to advertise that "... Phil Ochs had already confirmed his attendance". [42]

In an article published by Rolf Gekeler in the German magazine *Song*, [43] he expressed surprise that "... those outstanding voices of the younger generation, who years ago celebrated their first great successes in Newport and who gave the festival its legendary reputation as a 'mecca of folk song', are no longer there." [44] And noted: "The protagonists of the 'protest generation' no longer sing in Newport."

Quite critically Geleker stated further: "The young songwriters have gone into a kind of inner emigration. [...] At the moment the desire for security and love is more important to them than all political questions. [...] The younger generation of singers in America has replaced arguments and discussions, protests against contemporary issues by feelings, happiness and the symbol of all-encompassing love, the flower."

Gekeler's criticism is little surprising considering that Newport had always been a model and a source of inspiration for the Waldeck festivals. Also, the orientation of the Waldeck festivals was still far from the apolitical "... pseudo-cultures of flower-waving hippies" as Gekeler noted rather smugly.

The withdrawal from politics, that had already begun in the USA, and about which Phil Ochs would rather vehemently be complaining in the following years, at this point had not yet happened in Germany. The atmosphere was getting tense and the political events wouldn't go unnoticed at Waldeck.

Not only the orientation of the Waldeck festivals, which in their entire history had always considered themselves a forum for undogmatic political discussions, was quite openly questioned by left groups this year, but also the meaning of music and musicians as catalyst and carriers of political actions.

A *Basisgruppe Waldeck-Festival* (Waldeck festival action group), which mainly consisted of student groups from various university towns, stated in an appeal that was published and read during the festival, that the Waldeck festival no longer had any political significance and had "become a meeting for singing blinkered specialists". They further noted that: "Singers are no longer needed for revolutionary actions. Nowadays at sit-ins, go-ins and teach-ins singing has been aptly replaced by discussions with the intent of concrete action. [...] If the festival is still to have a serious political meaning, instead of major concerts, teach-ins about the specific problems of the antiauthoritarian movement will have to be held. So: Put the guitars aside and start discussing!" [45]

Their leaflet also called for a go-in at the Degenhardt concert that was to take place on the evening of Saturday the 15th of June. On this evening, Phil Ochs was to appear alongside Walter Mossmann.

There had already been disturbances the day before, amongst others, during the performances of songwriter Reinhard Mey and singer and cabaret artist Hanns Dieter Hüsch. Years later Hüsch described the events as "...a small literary show trial. This rude group of anarchists believed that they had to proclaim the cultural revolution [...] meanwhile all the liberal-minded artists should shut up and there would only be singing after there had been enough discussions." [46]

According to an article in the Swedish newspaper *Svenska Dagbladet,* Phil Ochs arrived at the Waldeck festival – with his brother Michael – right after a concert in Göteborg on the 12th of June. [47] At the time it was still so cold that Colin Wilkie, better prepared for the weather in the Hunsrück, had to lend some of his extra sweaters to the Ochs brothers, who were used to Californian temperatures. [48]

Phil's participation in an instrumental music workshop was scheduled for the morning of Thursday, the 13th of June. The very next day he was on stage for a performance at 4 p.m. This concert was announced as "Phil Ochs, Workshop: Topical Song-Writing in the USA". [49]

Even though the festival news of the 16th of June still declared: "Waldeck in the rain [...] the festival grounds are drenched, [...], the mood is drifting [...] the marquee: exceedingly crowded. Rain rattles guitar sounds..." [50], the weather seems to have been good during Phil's performance. In any case, he was standing on the open-air stage, blinking in the sun and singing his songs, undisturbed by disruptions and in front of an obviously rather relaxed audience. [51] This doesn't look like a classic workshop, but Michael Ochs had already pointed out that his brother preferred to do an entire concert of his own compositions. [52]

The Phil Ochs, Walter Mossmann and Franz-Josef Degenhardt evening concerts scheduled for Saturday became the real political issue.
According to the festival program, Ochs was to go on stage at 5:30 p.m., followed by performances of Mossmann and Degenhardt. The final concert by Insterburg & Co. was to take place at 11 p.m. [53]
The *Basisgruppe Waldeck-Festival* had called for a go-in at the Degenhardt concert "to turn it into a teach-in" coupled with the demand for Degenhardt to "make a statement" about the previously formulated theses.
The concerts were to take place in the marquee and apparently attendance numbers must have been quite sizeable. As stated in a contemporary report, "already an hour before the evening function started there was no room left in the big tent." [54] For that reason, and also due to the audience's enthusiasm for discussion, the start of Phil Ochs' concert was obviously delayed. A newspaper report describes the course of action and the heated atmosphere: "Before even Phil Ochs could begin, two Vietcong flags and a red flag were mounted on the back wall of the tent. Immediately the audience split again into two camps. After a lot of discussion and a fight for the flags, Franz-Josef Degenhardt exercised his authority stating: 'Comrades. If the flags don't stay, we won't sing.' Thus the fight was decided in favour of the radicals, the evening could begin." [55]

Existing sound recordings also suggest that Ochs had to struggle to start the concert at all and, at least at first, there was tremendous unrest in the audience. Obviously Phil got his audience under control, since all sources agree that his concert – like that of the other American singers – was held without interference. [56]

Both Mossmann and Degenhardt radically shortened their performances to give the audience the opportunity for discussion. [57] Eckhardt Holler presented the theses he had written, which had previously been distributed to the audience. Apparently they were not entirely well received, according to contemporary accounts part of the audience reacted with boos and shrill whistles. Preserved sound recordings also confirm that the approval was, by no means, undivided. [58] In any case, there was a heated discussion afterwards. However, later in the evening the performance of the comedy group Insterburg & Co. surprisingly managed to provide cheerfulness and relaxation.

Asked by the organisers for his personal opinion on the incidents in the marquee, Phil explained, "... that his political self approved the re-functioning of the event. It should, however, have been much wittier and shorter. 'The revolution catches up with the revolution of the songmakers'. And incidentally, he was about to write a song on the subject." [59]

It is easy to imagine that Phil Ochs, who was used to Yippie tactics from the US and familiar with the concept of the theatre of the absurd, would have expected more wit from the German would-be revolutionaries. He himself addressed it in the announcement to his song *The War is Over*: "I believe in militancy masked with some imagination rather than straight brawn. One of the things I've been trying to do in America is to get a lot of people to declare the war over in Vietnam. Just declare it over, from the bottom up..." [60] In two demonstrations, organised by Phil Ochs in Los Angeles and New York the previous year, he and his fellow protesters had done just that, armed with posters and all sorts of noisemakers they ran through the

streets loudly announcing that the war in Vietnam was over, to the disbelief and pleasant surprise of passers-by.
The underlying concept was explained by Phil himself: "The times demand a positive approach to demonstrations, a pro-life, joyful, energised, magnificently absurd demonstration against the sucking vacuum of war. [...] It's time for aesthetic rebellion, for creative anarchy; time for the use of surreal humor to ask now what our country is doing." [61]

Walter Mossmann, who had performed on the same evening as Phil and who was an admirer of his music, remembered in his memoirs a brief encounter in which they sat together while Ochs played *Crucifixion* and talked about Robert Kennedy, but strangely to him he had appeared "indifferent". [62]
In response to the disturbances during the previous concerts, a number of artists declared in a text read by Colin Wilkie that they would not perform under the given circumstances. After some discussion, however, the concerts and workshops scheduled for Sunday afternoon did take place after all. [63]
On Sunday, and for that matter, the last day of the Waldeck festival – only a final concert and press conference were scheduled for Monday – discussions and reflections about the festival already started. It was agreed – at least by the group debating about the festival – "that neither pure agitprop training nor simple artistic enjoyment ought to be the purpose of the festival in the future". Also more analysis and discussion about the musical performances, involving the artists and the audience, was recommended. [64]
Furthermore, on Sunday evening there was a vote on a resolution of solidarity for the striking French students. Of the two existing drafts, the one that regarded the "primary function" of the Waldeck festival as "being part of the international resistance centres" prevailed. [65]
After the end of the festival on Monday, the 17th of June, a "cross-section concert" of some Waldeck artists was planned for the evening in the Congress Hall in Frankfurt. Phil Ochs also participated

in this concert; other artists included Odetta, Colin Wilkie & Shirley Hart, as well as the German group Floh de Cologne, among others.

Months before, Rolf Gekeler had already "... requested timely notice from all interested parties who wanted to organise a concert with these two singers [i.e. Phil Ochs and Guy Carawan]" in the music magazine *Song*. "*Song* primarily considers the assistance of youth organisations, trade unions, student associations, folk and political clubs." [66] This was how Phil's follow-up concerts in Germany came about, the concert in Mönchengladbach, for instance, was organised by the "Waldecker" Peer Krolle. It was held at the Mathematics and Natural Sciences Grammar School, and next to Phil, Odetta once again appeared, though, she arrived late, since both she and her bass player had difficulties finding their way, so Phil had to sing for longer than expected. [67]

Another concert took place at the Technical University (TU) in Berlin where, on the 23rd of June, Phil performed again alongside Odetta. At a concert in Karlsruhe on the 24th he was joined by Guy Carawan, Colin Wilkie & Shirley Hart among others. [68]

On the Waldeck, however, the turbulent 1968 festival should have repercussions.

A general meeting was scheduled for the 30th of October. On the evening before, the council of elders had already assembled to discuss the consequences of the festival. It was concluded that "the original idea [....] had been overshadowed by certain political contents and 'concomitant circumstances' full of intolerance had led to unqualified discussions, thus the organisers had lost control of the management of the course of events. No longer *the song*, but rather the 'turmoil' dominated matters." [69]

There were also complaints about the high expenses which by far had exceeded the revenue. In particular the high cost of the flights for the American artists was criticised. Schneider stated that the festival had made a loss of 4,500 Deutschmark (DM), the travel expenses for the American singers alone already amounted to 20,000 DM. [70] The council of elders inferred that the idea of holding other festivals was not to be abandoned altogether, but declared that "...for a start the event was to be suspended in 1969."

In a corresponding statement, the organisers drew attention to the cultural value that the Waldeck festivals had already achieved and declared that incidents, such as those at the 1968 festival, had taken place throughout the year "...in all places where intellectually minded young people meet." Nevertheless, the festival "...had essentially very much been under the sign of *the song*..." and "excesses were properly handled." [71]

At the general meeting no final decision was taken on the festival's continuation. Instead, a working group was established to develop a concept on how a future festival could be designed. This working group, which consisted of younger "Waldeckers", did indeed present the board with a concept, which they, however, rejected. Although it was noted that the ABW could be proud of having conceived and realised the festivals, it was determined that the work of the association should not be limited to organising such an annual festival. Nonetheless, the possibility to make the site of the Waldeck available for a festival the following year, if other organisers stepped in, was explicitly left open. "Friendly youth groups with special care for the cause of the festival..." were who they principally had in mind. [72]

The sixth and last festival took place in 1969 from Wednesday, the 10th, to Sunday, the 14th of September, under the motto "Waldeck 69 – Gegenkultur" (Waldeck 69 – Counterculture).

For the first time, the ABW was no longer the organiser of the festival. Responsible was instead a *Waldeck project group* of 18 people, which, however, also included some younger members of the ABW, such as Ingo Weihe and Rolf Gekeler.

There were still far more than 2000 participants [73], even if the concept was to give more importance to lectures, discussions and workshops rather than to the music. At any rate, the music that was performed had also changed. This time around folk, chansons and protest songs only played a minor role, electrically amplified bands, which considered themselves as progressive, like Xhol Caravan, Checkpoint Charly, Amon Düül or Tangerine Dream, took a broader space. Long-standing Waldeck performers such as Hannes Wader and Reinhard Mey still appeared, but Hüsch and Süverkrüp didn't even attend, Degenhardt only payed a short visit and Mossmann held some workshops. The fragmentation of the student movement into many competing political groups as well as a retreat into drug experiments and an intensified inwardness also manifested itself on the Waldeck.

Therefore, the conclusions which the project group drew after the 1969 festival were also mixed. The differences between the various subcultures seemed too great. It was inferred to continue the debate, but no longer within the context of the Waldeck festivals. [74]

Larger music festivals on the Waldeck were not held again until the summer of 1993. [75]

Phil Ochs' last concert as part of his European tour was his performance in Mönchengladbach on the 25th of June. Afterwards, he travelled to England for a private stay but was almost prevented from entering the country by immigration officials. He was suspected of wanting to perform in England without a work permit. After some back and forth he was finally allowed to enter the country. Later apparently Phil had plans to visit Paris before returning to the US. [76]

Even though Phil Ochs was not to return for any more concerts in Germany, the experiences he made on the Waldeck seem to have stayed with him. In an article, published by Jerry Rubin in the American underground newspaper *Berkeley Barb* in early August 1968, he described how he and other Yippies had wanted to disturb the Newport Folk Festival with tactics similar to those used by the German SDS during a festival in Germany. [77] This festival, unspecified by Rubin, was, of course, the Waldeck festival and none other than Phil could have told him about it.

Here is Jerry Rubin's verbatim report: "This was all ironical because six Yippies and myself had come to Newport to disrupt the Folk Festival. We were inspired by what German SDS did to German left-wing singers at a festival last month in Germany. Midway through the concert SDS jumped on stage and took over the microphone. They called it a 'bourgeois festival' and said that people were consuming protest songs the way they consume clothes. 'The times are too revolutionary for this.' one said. After an hour of debate with the audience, they left and the concert continued amidst NLF flags and huge pictures of Ho Chi Minh. The Yippies came to Newport with similar ideas, but with no specific plan." [78]

Shortly after his return from Chicago in 1968, Phil also mentioned his experiences in an interview with Izzy Young. On the question as to which extent "writing songs" could support the youth movement, Phil answered with very little optimism: "I'm not sure that they can. The radical German students think that it's past that stage. The songs aren't enough obviously." [79]

As a singer who wanted to make a difference with his songs, the experiences on the Waldeck, the questioning of the relevance and effectiveness of political songs and their exponents, must have preoccupied Phil. [80]

Even in 1971, Phil still mentioned the events: "In 1968, when I played in Germany, I was told by the radical students that the kind of protest song I did was irrelevant to them. They were interested in action." [81]

The Waldeck festivals were history, but to a certain extent the events that took place there seem to have had an after-effect and left their mark on Phil Ochs.

Arbeitsgemeinschaft
Burg Waldeck e.V.
5449 Dorweiler
über Kastellaun
(Hunsrück)

Postscheck Köln 229825
Telephon (06762) 666

Chanson Folklore International

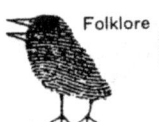

ABW E.V. 5449 DORWEILER/HSR.

Festival "CHANSON - FOLKLORE - INTERNATIONAL V
LIED 68
12. - 17. June 1968

I would like to participate in the 1968 festival at Waldeck castle in the Hunsrück.

Name: PHIL OCHS

Address: 1697 BROADWAY Rm. 1207, NEW YORK, N.Y., 1001 U.S.A.

Telephone: (212) 247-5733

I would like the following accomodation:
PRIVATE APARTMENT PER ~~LETT~~ LETTER

I do (not) intend to do a workshop (see information for participants).

Theme/duration:

Arbeitsgemeinschaft
Burg Waldeck e.V.
5449 Dorweiler
über Kastellaun
(Hunsrück)
Postscheck Köln 229825
Telephon (06762) 666

Chanson   Folklore   International

– 2 –

ABW. E.V. 5449 DORWEILER/HSR.

During the public concerts I shall sing:
Title of the song- state contents of foreign songs!
Duration, author and composer of each song:

Not decided at this time; however, Phil will sing songs of his own composition. Also, Phil would prefer to do a full concert.

The Arbeitsgemeinschaft Burg Waldeck as the organizer of CHANS
FOLKLORE – INTERNATIONAL V at Burg Waldeck is not in the pos:
to pay royalties of any kind to the participants.

The participants agree that the Arbeitsgemeinschaft Burg Walde(
guarantees to radio- and television companies the recording a⋅⋅
emmission of cross-section programmes from CHANSON –FOLKLORE
INTERNATIONAL and within this frame transfer to them all rights
of authorship, adaption and interpretation ect. of the songs. The
royalties paid by the radio- and television companies to the
Arbeitsgemeinschaft Burg Waldeck for casting cross-sections o:
festival – two at the maximum – will be used exclusively to m⋅:
expenses in connection with the festival.

Should participants and radio- and television companies present
come to any agreement exeeding the agreement made concerning t'
cross-section programme, the Arbeitsgemeinschaft Burg Waldeck a⋅t
as an agent.

Signature

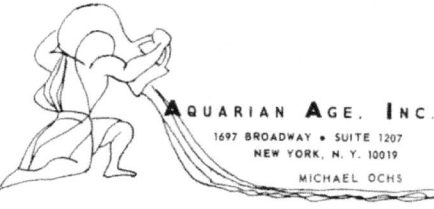

AQUARIAN AGE, INC.
1697 BROADWAY • SUITE 1207
NEW YORK, N. Y. 10019

MICHAEL OCHS   (212) 247-5733

May 22, 1968

Mr. Rolf Gekeler
852 Erlangen
Friedrichstr. 51
Western Germany

Dear Mr. Gekeler,

I am returning to you the contracts for the Berg Waldeck Festival and confirming The concerts at Munich and Frankfort. Phil would also like to play Berlin on one of his free dates, but he will not have time to do an extensive concert tour of Germany. After the Frankfort concert on June 17th, Phil will be going to France for two days (The 18th and 19th), then to Copenhagen for two days (the 20th and 21th), then the Concert in Munich (the 22nd), then he will go to England until July 7th. The best possible dates for a Berlin concert therefore, would be either June 20th or June 23rd. However, for a good Berlin concert, Phil would be willing to return to Germany later. If you need any additional information, etc, please write. Thank you.

Regards,

Michael Ochs

MO/re

Aquarian Age , Inc.
1697 Broadway Suite 12o7
N e w Y o r k N.Y. 1oo 19

Dear Mike,

Thank you for your letter. and the contracts.
In addition to Munich and Frankfurt a.M. at this time, we have
arranged additional concerts in the following cities on the
following dates: Karlsruhe 24.6. and M. Gladbach (near Düsseld
25.6.1968. We are negotiating for additional concerts, includ
Berlin , for three more concerts to follow München- Gladbach.
Please confirm M.- Gladbach and Karlsruhe dates by cable immed
I will advise you on Wednesday next,wof any additional concert
and dates.
Please send me the english lyrics of Phil's songs so that I
can translate them into German for The Radio and Press.
Please send Air - Express direct to Burg Waldeck.

Kindest regards

(Rolf Gekeler)   Dorweiler, Burg Waldeck   31-6-68

"The times have radicalism in the air." Gespräch mit Phil Ochs

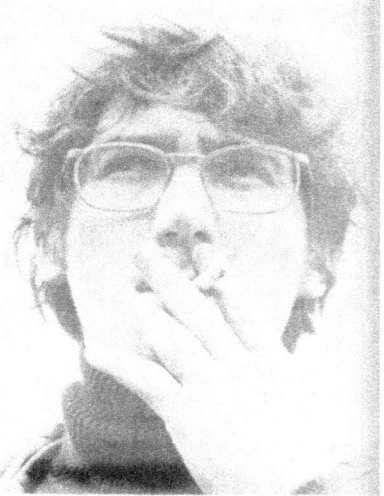

Über El Paso, Ohio und Virginia kam Phil Ochs Anfang der sechziger Jahre nach New York. Journalistik Studium an der Ohio State University hatte er abgebrochen, um Lieder zu schreiben und sie zu singen Beeinflußt von Presley, Buddy Holly, den Everly Brothers und dann dem Kingston Trio, Joan Baez, Seeger und Guthrie in dieser zeitlichen Reihenfolge, fing er an "topical songs" zu schreiben, das, was dann die Marke "Protest" aufgeklebt bekam. Ausgeschlossen von Massenmedien, später auch nicht mehr nach Newport eingeladen, zeigt sich auf seinen Platten und in seinen Konzerten der Wandel von Symptomkritik zu politischer Analyse, unterbrochen von einem romantischen Ausflug zu Blumenverkäuferinnen und Rauschgiftgebäck. Seit er im letzten Sommer eine Bewegung gründete, die den Krieg für beendet und diejenigen für verrückt erklärte, die ihn weiterführen, ist er wieder Teil der politischen Szene in den USA. Zur Zeit singt er, mit gehörigen Vorbehalten, im Wahlkampf Senator McCarthys. Auf einer Reise durch Skandinavien und Deutschland sang er für die amerikanischen Deserteure in Schweden, für französische Studenten, und war beeindruckt von der Studentenbewegung. Ausdrücklich solidarisierte er sich mit den Sängern und Teilnehmern am diesjährigen Waldeck Festival, die das Publikum zwangen, nicht nur zu konsumieren, sondern sich mit dem Gebotenen kritisch auseinanderzusetzen Die Song-Mitarbeiter Uwe J. Nagel und Volker Zinser interviewten Phil auf der Burg Waldeck.

song: Als Sie anfingen zu singen, wo standen Sie damals politisch?

Phil: Ich weiß nicht mehr genau, auf jeden Fall war ich für Kennedy. Dann kam Castro und die Invasion in der Schweinebucht. Die Invasion brachte mich weiter nach links, bisher hatte ich Castro feindlich gegenübergestanden, beeinflußt durch die Propaganda. Die Invasion zeigte die andere Seite. Politik zu diesem Zeitpunkt hieß, das amerikanische System zu reformieren. Ich stand immer noch unter dem Einfluß des kalten Krieges.

song: Ihre Lieder kritisierten nur Einzelheiten, Symptome. Doch dann kam z.B. "I ain't marching anymore" ein pazifistisches Lied. Sind Sie Pazifist?

Phil: Ja und Nein. Eine Art Pazifist. (lacht). Als ich älter wurde, erschien mir der Gedanke an die Existenz von Armeen immer lächerlicher. Ich glaube nicht, daß ich im Zweiten Weltkrieg Pazifist gewesen wäre. In Vietnam würde ich wahrscheinlich für den Vietcong kämpfen. Ich sehe nicht ein, weshalb ich jetzt kämpfen und sterben soll. Sicherlich hat das alles mit der spezifisch amerikanischen Armee zu tun.

song: Auf der dritten Platte singen Sie zum ersten Male über die Hintergründe der amerikanischen Außenpolitik, über Santo Domingo, Revolution

Phil: Ja, hier fing ich an, Zusammenhänge zu begreifen.

song: Und auf der Rückseite der Plattenhülle

Phil: waren Gedichte von Mao Tse Tung abgedruckt mit der Frage: "Ist das der Feind?" man bekam sie damals nirgendwo zu kaufen. Das war sowohl eine ästhetische Frage als auch eine politische, die etwas mit der Gehirnwäsche zu tun hatte, der die amerikanische Öffentlichkeit unterliegt. Es drehte sich um die Frage, ob dieser Mann wirklich so verrückt war, wie man ihn uns präsentierte.

song: Auf der Platte ist ein Lied, "Love me, I'm a liberal". Sind das eigene Erlebnisse, eine Selbstanalyse?

Phil: Ich bin mit dem Mann schon irgendwie identisch, ich fluktuiere da, aber nur in manchen Aspekten. Was mich maßlos empörte, war die Haltung der Liberalen beim Tode von Malcolm X, so "naja, er hat's ja nicht anders gewollt!" Das war der Höhepunkt meines Hasses gegen die Liberalen. Andererseits gibt es die Stevensons, Kennedies oder McCarthys, sogar Humphrey.

song: Das Grundproblem der amerikanischen Linken scheint das Fehlen einer sozialistischen Bewegung zu sein, wer etwas ändern will, muß zu den Liberalen.

Phil: Nun, es gab schon immer Sozialisten.

song: vor 80 Jahren

Phil: naja, es war und ist da, wenn auch nur als eine Art romantische Erinnerung, Henry Wallace, Norman Thomas. Die haben eine Basis gebaut, von der die Demokratische Partei sozialistische Ge-

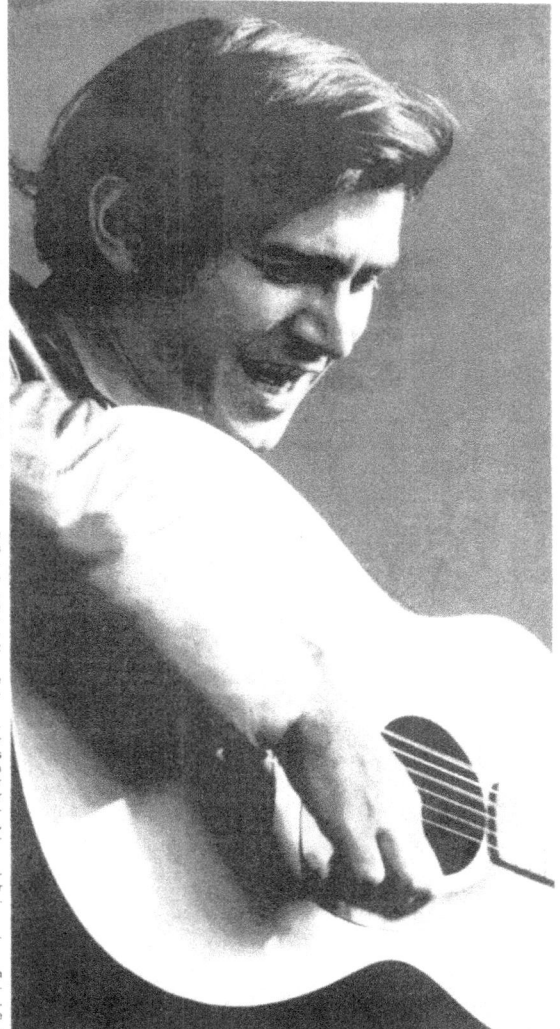

35

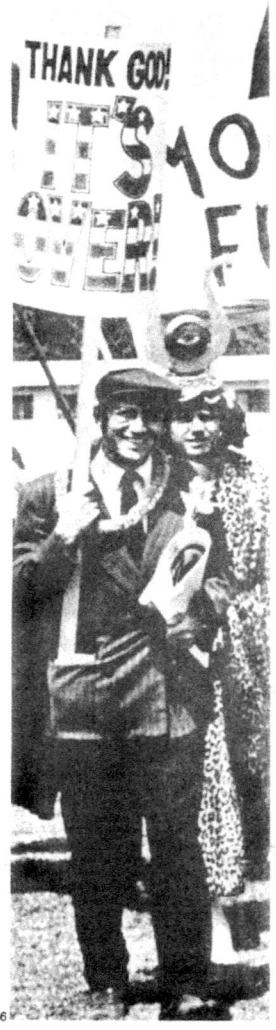

danken übernahm. Sozialversicherung, zum Beispiel. Die Partei hat immer versucht, die Linke heranzuziehen. Genau das tut heute McCarthy, der weiter gegangen ist, als die meisten "Liberalen" es tun würden. Außerdem ist er vertrauenswürdiger

song: Als Senator Kennedy?

Phil: Ganz bestimmt. Ich weiß nicht, ob der nicht ein besserer Präsident gewesen wäre, ich meine, als eine Art charismatischer Führer. Aber was Vertrauen anbelangt, ziehe ich McCarthy vor Radikalismus liegt in der Luft, das zeigt auch die guten Seiten der Liberalen. Humphrey natürlich ist völlig reaktionär geworden.

song: Nun, in Krisenzeiten sind die Liberalen immer völlig gespalten.

Phil: Genau, und diejenigen, die sich nach links bewegen, sind ziemlich brauchbare Leute. Ich glaube, das Establishment hier will im Augenblick wirklich eine Art Wandel. Sie spüren die Krise, und wenn es ihnen gelingt, zu verhindern, daß in Amerika etwas grundlegend geändert wird, dann werden sie sich außenpolitisch etwas zurückziehen. Hier wird McCarthy wichtig. Er ist kein Opportunist, scheint mir Er hat ein Buch geschrieben, "The Limits of Power" und nur der Idee, daß ein Präsidentschaftskandidat in einem Buch die "Grenzen der Macht" anspricht, scheint mir schon interessant. Ich halte ihn für unbedingt notwendig zu diesem Zeitpunkt. Gewinnt er nicht, kann es bald ein großes Blutbad geben.

song: Was bedeutet nun die Tatsache, daß Sie für McCarthy singen? Welche Funktion haben Sie?

Phil: Ich glaube definitiv, daß man mit Liedern politische Aussagen machen kann. Meine Rolle während des Wahlkampfes ist eigenartig, bis heute habe ich McCarthy noch nicht voll unterstützt, immer nur Teile seines Programms. Ich sage immer er sei noch ein Politiker des kalten Krieges. Ich weise auf Dinge hin, die McCarthy nicht erwähnt, wie Polizeibrutalität, die Tätigkeit von Jim Garrisson, dem einzigen amerikanischen Staatsanwalt, der den Warren Report anzweifelt usw. Ich sang in Madison Square Garden vor 20.000 Menschen "Love me, I'm a liberal" und sagte: "Ich hoffe, daß der Wahlkampf nicht zu einer solchen Form von Liberalismus degeneriert" Er läßt sich von jungen Leuten beeinflussen, von seinen Töchtern. Während seines wirklich ungewöhnlichen Wahlkampfes hat er als erster den Rücktritt von Hoover gefordert und das ist ein grosser Schritt in die richtige Richtung. Hoover ist das Kernstück des Faschismus in den USA, der absolute Kern, seit Jahrzehnten fürchten ihn die Präsidenten, inklusive Kennedy. Dann hat McCarthy auch gesagt, er würde auch dann die Truppen aus Vietnam zurückziehen, wenn Friedensgespräche erfolglos wären — das hat noch niemand außer ihm gesagt (gemeint sind die anderen Kandidaten, die Red.). Wichtig ist seine Persönlichkeit, er ist kein "Führer" alles an ihm ist Understatement. Aus diesem Grund halten ihn die Massenmedien nicht für einen Mann, der "stark" genug ist, um das Land zu regieren. Als letztes, McCarthy ist wichtig als Erzieher für eine Öffentlichkeit, die jahrelanger Gehirnwäsche unterlag. Er ist wie eine Art guter Onkel (everybody's favourite English teacher), der sagt: "Nun, im Grunde genommen müssen wir das doch gar nicht tun, in Lateinamerika, in Südostasien." Dann gibt es natürlich die radikalere Position. Man will, daß Humphrey gewinnt, um dann links und rechts zu polarisieren. Ich versuche, diese Position weitgehend zu vermeiden. Wenn noch ein Funken Vernunft in der Politik steckt, wird McCarthy Präsident, wenn nicht, kann das nur tödlich enden (will explode into death).

song: Also haben Sie noch Hoffnung?

Phil: Nun, mehr die Hoffnung der Verzweiflung. Ich habe ernsthafte Zweifel.

song: Zurück zu Ihren Liedern. Nach drei Platten mit "topical songs" kam Pleasures of the Harbour (POH), Sie gingen nach Californien. Weshalb?

Phil: Nach "Changes" besonders wollte ich einige lyrische, mehr philosophische Lieder schreiben, ich wollte etwas völlig anderes machen. "Changes" ist so ziemlich das schönste, was ich an Liedern schreiben kann, aber ich hatte Schwierigkeiten, es zu singen. Ich wollte eine Single herausbringen, ähnlich wie "Yesterday" und die Elektra-Leute sagten einfach "Nein" was mich maßlos wütend machte. Von dieser Wut zu POH war nur noch ein kleiner Schritt.

song: Ist das einer der Gründe, weshalb Sie Elektra verlassen haben und zu A&M gegangen sind?

Phil: Zur Zeit möchte ich darüber noch nicht sprechen. Nur soviel: mein Vertrag lief aus und in Anbetracht vieler Dinge ging ich zu A&M nach Californien.

song: Normalerweise wird man doch stark von seinem Milieu beeinflußt. Wieso kommt es, daß Sie die intellektuelle Atmosphäre New Yorks mit der von Los Angeles eintauschten, die doch nun wirklich das Zentrum einer reaktionären Mittelklasse ist?

Phil: Ohne Frage hat Californien eine bessere musikalische Atmosphäre als New York, bessere Studios, bessere Musiker etc. New York ist so aufgeblasen, vollgestopft mit "Intellektuellen" Vor 10 Jahren, als Dylan und ich noch dort waren, fühlte man sich wohler 1962, 1963. Politisch gesehen haben Sie recht. Los Angeles ist fast eine Karikatur der amerikanischen Mittelklasse. Doch gibt es Künstlerkolonien, Täler Canyons, in denen man gut leben kann. Californien ist so unterschiedlich, abenteuerlich, viele freaks leben dort.

song: Wurden Sie von der hippy Bewegung beeinflußt?

Phil: Nicht sehr Es schien nur so, als ob der Sommer 1967 unglaublich schön und aufregend werden würde, als ob die ganze Lebenskraft dorthin wollte. Irgendwie

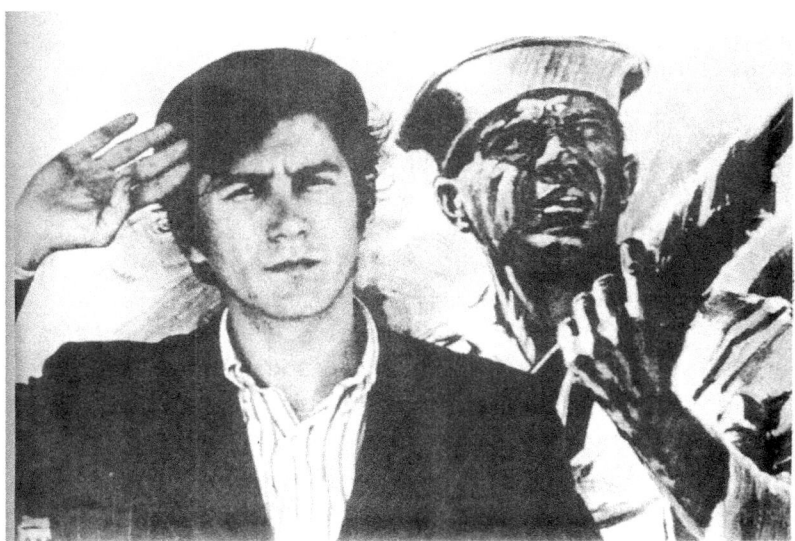

kam nur die Hälfte an, ich weiß nicht, wo die andere Hälfte blieb. Damals war die Bewegung noch nicht korrumpiert wie heute, jetzt ist sie völlig verfallen.

song: Wie groß ist der Einfluß von Pop-Gruppen auf Ihre Lieder?

Phil: Zweifellos gibt es Einflüsse der Beatles, der Stones, die ich beide sehr schätze. Ich habe genaue Vorstellungen von Strömungen in der Musik (life forces in music), folk music erreichte einen wunderbaren Höhepunkt 1963, 1964, vielleicht 1965. Dann kam der Übergang von folk zu folk-rock und pop, 65 war musikalisch ein großartiges Jahr Aftermath, Rubber Soul

song: Dylan ging nach England —

Phil: auch Dylan hatte seinen Höhepunkt erreicht, Tim Hardin, Donavan, alles schien voranzugehen, positiv, dann kam der Verfall 1966, 1967 Psychedelische Musik stellte sich als Fehlschlag heraus.

song: Das Dilemma war ja letztes Jahr in Newport zu sehen. Die Leute, die bis dahin naiv "Protest" betrieben und Symptome kritisiert hatten, ohne sich die Mühe zu machen, wirklich politische Analysen zu betreiben, waren auf Grund der Fehlschläge frustriert und stürzten sich auf "love" Nicht nur Sie waren nicht eingeladen worden, auch Len Chandler nicht oder Janis Ian, deren vergleichsweise harmlosen Lieder doch immer noch wichtiger gewesen wären als das, was von den anderen jungen Leuten gezeigt wurde.

Phil: Nun, ich nehme an, daß ich auch dieses Jahr nicht eingeladen werde, und das halte ich einfach für kindisch. Gut, 1967 war unpolitisch, man war sehr mit Rauschgift beschäftigt, aber dieses Jahr ist ein außerordentlich politisches Jahr Daß man keine guten politischen Sänger aufweisen kann, halte ich nicht nur für künstlerisches Versagen, sondern für eine Schande, wenn man den Verfall der Politik hier in Betracht zieht.

song: Und Ihre Europa-Reise?

Phil: Es ist außerordentlich gut verlaufen, wenn man das Sprachproblem mit einbezieht. wir hatten überall Diskussionen, zum Teil nach dem Konzert. Zudem trat ich im Fernsehen, auf der ich die Länder Skandinaviens aufforderte, die diplomatischen Beziehungen mit den USA abzubrechen. Die Zuhörer waren überall außerordentlich, das hat sicher mit der politischen Situation hier zu tun. Während ich von Revolution singe, machen sich die Leute sowieso schon Gedanken darüber in Frankreich, in Deutschland. Es ist ähnlich wie 1963, als die Bürgerrechtsbewegung ihren Höhepunkt hatte.

song: Pläne für die Zukunft?

Phil: Bevor ich nach Deutschland fuhr habe ich gerade zwei große Projekte beendet. Einmal meine fünfte Platte, "Tapes from California" die politisch der Konzertplatte ähnlich ist, musikalisch POH.

Sogar einige ganz traditionale Sachen wie "Joe Hill" das ich zusammen mit Jack Elliot singe — als eine super-folk Aufnahme (lacht). Die Platte ist für mich persönlich sehr wichtig, sie handelt vom geistigen und politischen Verfall Amerikas. Auf der Rückseite ist ein offener Brief:

Die NLF nagt
sie haben keine Angst
sie sind nicht allein.
Du hast Angst
Du bist allein.
Sollte der Befreiungskrieg
endlich nach Hause kommen?

So, wie die Konzertplatte versuchte, das Dilemma der amerikanischen Außenpolitik zu entlarven, soll diese Platte das Dilemma der amerikanischen Jugend aufzeigen. Wohin sollen wir gehen, gibt es eine Revolution, weshalb ist Amerika krank und was ist die Struktur der Krankheit, was bedeutet Krieg?

Zum zweiten habe ich gerade ein Buch herausgebracht mit den Liedern der letzten drei Platten, mit Gedichten, mit Artikeln über Dylan und die folk scene, über Newport, was sich in den Jahren so ergeben hat.

song: Danke schön.

Song, Nr. 7, 1968, S.34-37

"The times have radicalism in the air"
Gespräch mit Phil Ochs

Über El Paso, Ohio und Virginia kam Phil Ochs Anfang der sechziger Jahre nach New York. Journalistik Studium an der Ohio State University hatte er abgebrochen, um Lieder zu schreiben und sie zu singen. Beeinflußt von Presley, Buddy Holly, den Everly Brothers und dann dem Kingston Trio, Joan Baez, Seeger und Guthrie – in dieser zeitlichen Reihenfolge –, fing er an „topical songs" zu schreiben, das, was dann die Marke „Protest" aufgeklebt bekam. Ausgeschlossen von Massenmedien, später auch nicht mehr nach Newport eingeladen, zeigt sich auf seinen Platten und in seinen Konzerten der Wandel von Symptomkritik zu politischer Analyse, unterbrochen von einem romantischen Ausflug zu Blumenverkäuferinnen und Rauschgiftgebäck. Seit er im letzten Sommer eine Bewegung gründete, die den Krieg für beendet und diejenigen für verrückt erklärte, die ihn weiterführen, ist er wieder Teil der politischen Szene in den USA. Zur Zeit singt er, mit gehörigen Vorbehalten, im Wahlkampf Senator McCarthys. Auf einer Reise durch Skandinavien und Deutschland sang er für die amerikanischen Deserteure in Schweden, für französische Studenten, und war beeindruckt von der Studentenbewegung. Ausdrücklich solidarisierte er sich mit den Sängern und Teilnehmern am diesjährigen Waldeck Festival, die das Publikum zwangen, nicht nur zu konsumieren, sondern sich mit dem Gebotenen kritisch auseinanderzusetzen. Die *Song*-Mitarbeiter Uwe J. Nagel und Volker Zinser interviewten Phil auf der Burg Waldeck.

song: Als Sie anfingen zu singen, wo standen Sie damals politisch?

Phil: Ich weiß nicht mehr genau, auf jeden Fall war ich für Kennedy. Dann kam Castro und die Invasion in der Schweinebucht. Die Invasion brachte mich weiter nach links, bisher hatte ich Castro feindlich gegenübergestanden, beeinflußt durch die Propaganda. Die Invasion zeigte die andere Seite. Politik zu diesem Zeitpunkt hieß, das amerikanische System zu reformieren. Ich stand immer noch unter dem Einfluß des kalten Krieges.

song: Ihre Lieder kritisierten nur Einzelheiten, Symptome. Doch dann kam z.B. *I ain't marching anymore*, ein pazifistisches Lied. Sind Sie Pazifist?

Phil: Ja und Nein. Eine Art Pazifist. (lacht). Als ich älter wurde, erschien mir der Gedanke an die Existenz von Armeen immer lächerlicher. Ich glaube nicht, daß ich im Zweiten Weltkrieg Pazifist gewesen wäre. In Vietnam würde ich wahrscheinlich für den Vietcong kämpfen. Ich sehe nicht ein, weshalb ich jetzt kämpfen und sterben soll. Sicherlich hat das alles mit der spezifisch amerikanischen Armee zu tun.

song: Auf der dritten Platte singen Sie zum ersten Male über die Hintergründe der amerikanischen Außenpolitik, über Santo Domingo, Revolution ...

Phil: Ja, hier fing ich an, Zusammenhänge zu begreifen.

song: Und auf der Rückseite der Plattenhülle ...

Phil: ... waren Gedichte von Mao Tse Tung abgedruckt mit der Frage: „Ist das der Feind?", man bekam sie damals nirgendwo zu kaufen. Das war sowohl eine ästhetische Frage als auch eine politische, die etwas mit der Gehirnwäsche zu tun hatte, der die amerikanische Öffentlichkeit unterliegt. Es drehte sich um die Frage, ob dieser Mann wirklich so verrückt war, wie man ihn uns präsentierte.

song: Auf der Platte ist ein Lied, *Love me, I'm a Liberal*. Sind das eigene Erlebnisse, eine Selbstananalyse?

Phil: Ich bin mit dem Mann schon irgendwie identisch, ich fluktuiere da, aber nur in manchen Aspekten. Was mich maßlos empörte, war die Haltung der Liberalen beim Tode von Malcolm X, so „naja, er hat's ja nicht anders gewollt!". Das war der Höhepunkt meines Hasses gegen die Liberalen. Andererseits gibt es die Stevensons, Kennedys oder McCarthys, sogar Humphrey.

song: Das Grundproblem der amerikanischen Linken scheint das Fehlen einer sozialistischen Bewegung zu sein, wer etwas ändern will, muß zu den Liberalen.

Phil: Nun, es gab schon immer Sozialisten.

song: ... vor 80 Jahren ...

Phil: ... naja, es war und ist da, wenn auch nur als eine Art romantische Erinnerung, Henry Wallace, Norman Thomas. Die haben eine Basis gebaut, von der die Demokratische Partei sozialistische Gedanken übernahm. Sozialversicherung, zum Beispiel. Die Partei hat immer versucht, die Linke heranzuziehen. Genau das tut heute McCarthy, der weiter gegangen ist, als die meisten „Liberalen" es tun würden. Außerdem ist er vertrauenswürdiger.

song: Als Senator Kennedy?

Phil: Ganz bestimmt. Ich weiß nicht, ob der nicht ein besserer Präsident gewesen wäre, ich meine, als eine Art charismatischer Führer. Aber was Vertrauen anbelangt, ziehe ich McCarthy vor. Radikalismus liegt in der Luft, das zeigt auch die guten Seiten der Liberalen. Humphrey natürlich ist völlig reaktionär geworden.

song: Nun, in Krisenzeiten sind die Liberalen immer völlig gespalten.

Phil: Genau, und diejenigen, die sich nach links bewegen, sind ziemlich brauchbare Leute. Ich glaube, das Establishment hier will im Augenblick wirklich eine Art Wandel. Sie spüren die Krise, und wenn es ihnen gelingt, zu verhindern, daß in Amerika etwas grundlegend geändert wird, dann werden sie sich auch außenpolitisch etwas zurückziehen. Hier wird McCarthy wichtig. Er ist kein Opportunist, scheint mir. Er hat ein Buch geschrieben, "The

Limits of Power", und nur die Idee, daß ein Präsidentschaftskandidat in einem Buch die „Grenzen der Macht" anspricht, scheint mir schon interessant. Ich halte ihn für unbedingt notwendig zu diesem Zeitpunkt. Gewinnt er nicht, kann es bald ein großes Blutbad geben.

song: Was bedeutet nun die Tatsache, daß Sie für McCarthy singen? Welche Funktion haben Sie?

Phil: Ich glaube definitiv, daß man mit Liedern politische Aussagen machen kann. Meine Rolle während des Wahlkampfes ist eigenartig, bis heute habe ich McCarthy noch nicht voll unterstützt, immer nur Teile seines Programms. Ich sage immer, er sei noch ein Politiker des kalten Krieges. Ich weise auf Dinge hin, die McCarthy nicht erwähnt, wie Polizeibrutalität, die Tätigkeit von Jim Garrisson, dem einzigen amerikanischen Staatsanwalt, der den Warren Report anzweifelt usw. Ich sang im Madison Square Garden vor 20.000 Menschen *Love me, I'm a Liberal* und sagte: „Ich hoffe, daß der Wahlkampf nicht zu einer solchen Form von Liberalismus degeneriert." Er läßt sich von jungen Leuten beeinflussen, von seinen Töchtern. Während seines wirklich ungewöhnlichen Wahlkampfes hat er als erster den Rücktritt von Hoover gefordert und das ist ein großer Schritt in die richtige Richtung. Hoover ist das Kernstück des Faschismus in den USA, der absolute Kern, seit Jahrzehnten fürchten ihn die Präsidenten, inklusive Kennedy. Dann hat McCarthy auch gesagt, er würde auch dann die Truppen aus Vietnam zurückziehen, wenn Friedensgespräche erfolglos wären – das hat noch niemand außer ihm gesagt [gemeint sind die anderen Kandidaten, die Red.]. Wichtig ist seine Persönlichkeit, er ist kein „Führer", alles an ihm ist Understatement. Aus diesem Grund halten ihn die Massenmedien nicht für einen Mann, der „stark" genug ist, um das Land zu regieren. Als letztes, McCarthy ist wichtig als Erzieher für eine Öffentlichkeit, die jahrelanger Gehirnwäsche unterlag. Er ist wie eine Art guter Onkel (everybody's favourite English teacher), der sagt: „Nun, im Grunde genommen müssen wir das doch gar nicht tun, in Lateinamerika, in Südostasien." Dann gibt es natürlich die radikalere Position. Man will, daß Humphrey gewinnt, um dann links und rechts zu polarisieren. Ich versuche, diese Position weitgehend zu vermeiden. Wenn noch ein Funken Vernunft in der Politik steckt, wird McCarthy Präsident, wenn nicht, kann das nur tödlich enden (will explode into death).

song: Also haben Sie noch Hoffnung?

Phil: Nun, mehr die Hoffnung der Verzweiflung. Ich habe ernsthafte Zweifel.

song: Zurück zu Ihren Liedern. Nach drei Platten mit „topical songs" kam *Pleasures of the Harbor (POH),* Sie gingen nach Californien. Weshalb?

Phil: Nach *Changes* besonders wollte ich einige lyrische, mehr philosophische Lieder schreiben, ich wollte etwas völlig anderes machen. *Changes* ist so ziemlich das schönste, was ich an Liedern schreiben kann, aber ich hatte Schwierigkeiten, es zu singen. Ich wollte eine Single herausbringen, ähnlich wie *Yesterday,* und die Elektra-Leute sagten einfach „Nein", was mich maßlos wütend machte. Von dieser Wut zu *POH* war nur noch ein kleiner Schritt.

song: Ist das einer der Gründe, weshalb Sie Elektra verlassen haben und zu A&M gegangen sind?

Phil: Zur Zeit möchte ich darüber noch nicht sprechen. Nur soviel: mein Vertrag lief aus und in Anbetracht vieler Dinge ging ich zu A&M nach Californien.

song: Normalerweise wird man doch stark von seinem Milieu beeinflußt. Wieso kommt es, daß Sie die intellektuelle Atmosphäre New Yorks mit der von Los Angeles eintauschten, die doch nun wirklich das Zentrum einer reaktionären Mittelklasse ist?

Phil: Ohne Frage hat Californien eine bessere musikalische Atmosphäre als New York, bessere Studios, bessere Musiker etc. New York ist so aufgeblasen, vollgestopft mit „Intellektuellen". Vor 10 Jahren, als Dylan und ich noch dort waren, fühlte man sich wohler, 1962, 1963. Politisch gesehen haben Sie recht. Los Angeles ist fast eine Karikatur der amerikanischen Mittelklasse. Doch gibt es

Künstlerkolonien, Täler, Canyons, in denen man gut leben kann. Californien ist so unterschiedlich, abenteuerlich, viele Freaks leben dort.

song: Wurden Sie von der Hippie Bewegung beeinflußt?

Phil: Nicht sehr. Es schien nur so, als ob der Sommer 1967 unglaublich schön und aufregend werden würde, als ob die ganze Lebenskraft dorthin wollte. Irgendwie kam nur die Hälfte an, ich weiß nicht, wo die andere Hälfte blieb. Damals war die Bewegung noch nicht korrumpiert wie heute, jetzt ist sie völlig verfallen.

song: Wie groß ist der Einfluß von Pop-Gruppen auf Ihre Lieder?

Phil: Zweifellos gibt es Einflüsse der Beatles, der Stones, die ich beide sehr schätze. Ich habe genaue Vorstellungen von Strömungen in der Musik (life forces in music), folk music erreichte einen wunderbaren Höhepunkt 1963, 1964, vielleicht 1965. Dann kam der Übergang von folk zu folk-rock und pop, '65 war musikalisch ein großartiges Jahr, *Aftermath, Rubber Soul* ...

song: Dylan ging nach England –

Phil: ... auch Dylan hatte seinen Höhepunkt erreicht, Tim Hardin, Donovan, alles schien voranzugehen, positiv, dann kam der Verfall 1966, 1967. Psychedelische Musik stellte sich als Fehlschlag heraus.

song: Das Dilemma war ja letztes Jahr in Newport zu sehen. Die Leute, die bis dahin naiv „Protest" betrieben und Symptome kritisiert hatten, ohne sich die Mühe zu machen, wirklich politische Analysen zu betreiben, waren auf Grund der Fehlschläge frustriert und stürzten sich auf „love". Nicht nur Sie waren nicht eingeladen worden, auch Len Chandler nicht oder Janis Ian, deren vergleichsweise harmlose Lieder doch immer noch wichtiger gewesen wären als das, was von den anderen jungen Leuten gezeigt wurde.

Phil: Nun, ich nehme an, daß ich auch dieses Jahr nicht eingeladen werde, und das halte ich einfach für kindisch. Gut, 1967 war unpolitisch, man war sehr mit Rauschgift beschäftigt, aber dieses

Jahr ist ein außerordentlich politisches Jahr. Daß man keine guten politischen Sänger aufweisen kann, halte ich nicht nur für künstlerisches Versagen, sondern für eine Schande, wenn man den Verfall der Politik hier in Betracht zieht.

song: Und Ihre Europa-Reise?

Phil: Ist außerordentlich gut verlaufen, wenn man das Sprachproblem mit einbezieht. Wir hatten überall Diskussionen, zum Teil nach dem Konzert. Zudem trat ich im Fernsehen auf, was mir in den USA verwehrt wird. Ich hatte eine Pressekonferenz im Fernsehen, auf der ich die Länder Skandinaviens aufforderte, die diplomatischen Beziehungen mit den USA abzubrechen. Die Zuhörer waren überall außerordentlich, das hat sicher mit der politischen Situation hier zu tun. Während ich von Revolution singe, machen sich die Leute sowieso schon Gedanken darüber, in Frankreich, in Deutschland. Es ist ähnlich wie 1963, als die Bürgerrechtsbewegung ihren Höhepunkt hatte.

song: Pläne für die Zukunft?

Phil: Bevor ich nach Deutschland fuhr, habe ich gerade zwei große Projekte beendet. Einmal meine fünfte Platte, *Tape from California,* die politisch der Konzertplatte ähnlich ist, musikalisch *POH*. Sogar einige ganz traditionelle Sachen wie *Joe Hill,* das ich zusammen mit Jack Elliot singe – als eine super-folk Aufnahme (lacht). Die Platte ist für mich persönlich sehr wichtig, sie handelt vom geistigen und politischen Verfall Amerikas. Auf der Rückseite ist ein offener Brief:

Die NLF nagt
sie haben keine Angst,
sie sind nicht allein.
Du hast Angst,
Du bist allein.
Sollte der Befreiungskrieg
endlich nach Hause kommen?

So, wie die Konzertplatte versuchte, das Dilemma der amerikanischen Außenpolitik zu entlarven, soll diese Platte das Dilemma der amerikanischen Jugend aufzeigen. Wohin sollen wir gehen, gibt es eine Revolution, weshalb ist Amerika krank und was ist die Struktur der Krankheit, was bedeutet der Krieg?

Zum zweiten habe ich gerade ein Buch herausgebracht mit den Liedern der letzten drei Platten, mit Gedichten, mit Artikeln über Dylan und die folk scene, über Newport, was sich in den Jahren so ergeben hat.

song: Danke schön.

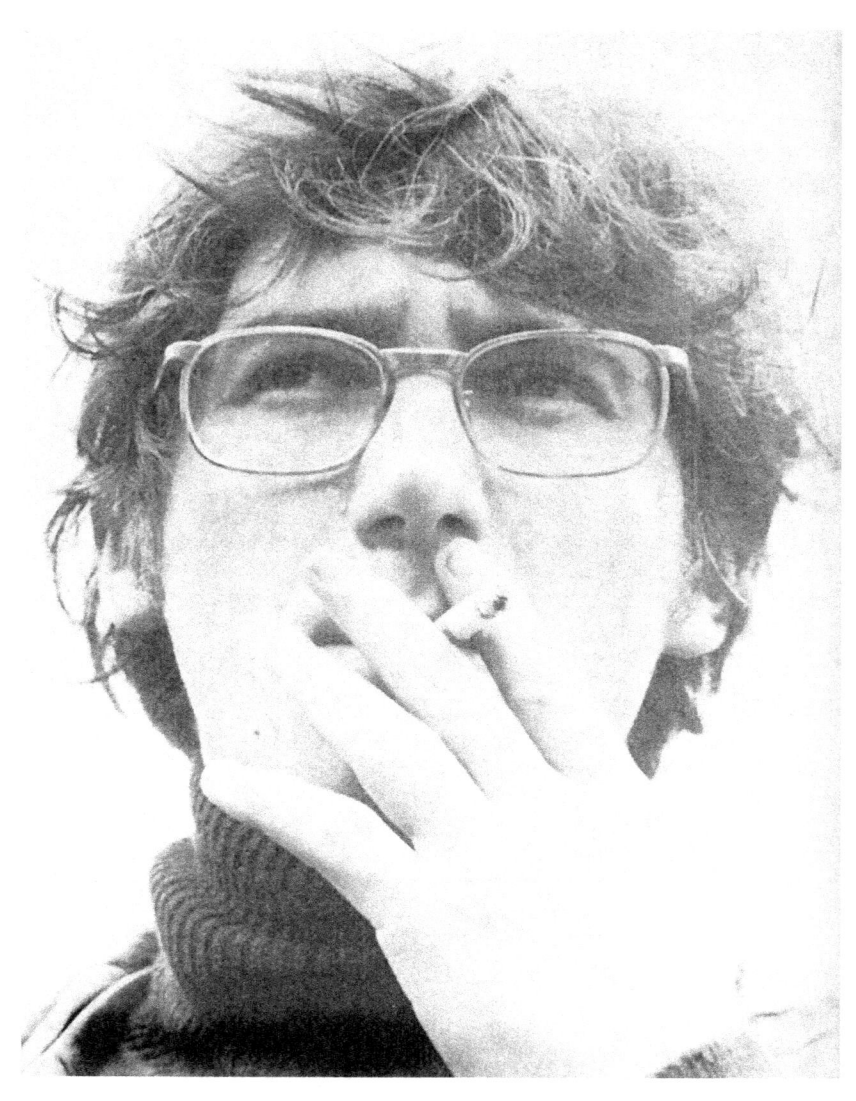

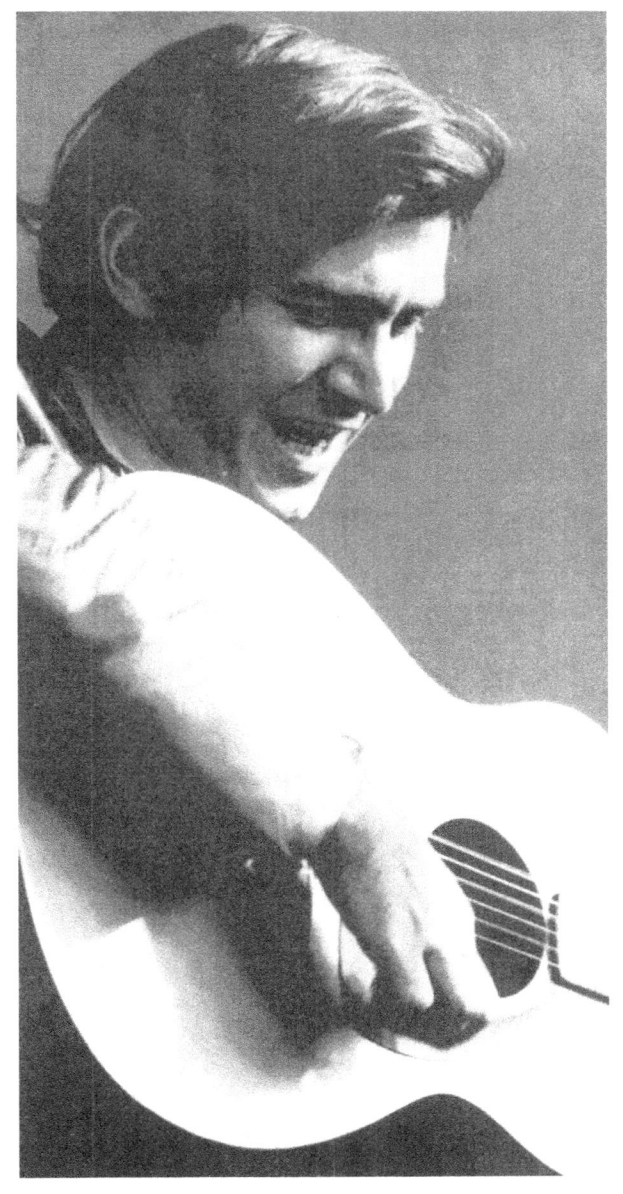

"The times have radicalism in the air"
Interview with Phil Ochs

In the early sixties Phil Ochs came to New York via El Paso, Ohio and Virginia. He gave up his journalism studies at the Ohio State University in favour of writing songs and singing them. Influenced by Presley, Buddy Holly, the Everly Brothers and later on the Kingston Trio, Joan Baez, Seeger and Guthrie – in this sequence – he started writing "topical songs" which were then labelled "protest". Excluded from the mass media, later also no longer invited to Newport, his records and concerts clearly show the change from criticism of symptoms to political analysis, interrupted by a romantic excursion to flower selling girls and drug cookies. Last summer he founded a movement which declared the war as being over and those who continue it as insane. Since that time he has again become part of the political scene in the USA. At present he sings, however, with a good deal of reservations in Senator McCarthy's election campaign. During a tour through Scandinavia and Germany he sang in favour of American deserters in Sweden, in favour of French students and showed himself impressed by the student movement. He explicitly showed solidarity with the singers and participants of this year's Waldeck festival who forced the audience not merely to consume, but also to look critically at the presentations. Two members of the *Song* team, Uwe J. Nagel and Volker Zinser interviewed Phil on the Burg Waldeck.

song: Where did you stand politically at the time you started to sing?

Phil: I do not really remember, but anyway I was pro Kennedy. Then Castro came and the Bay of Pigs Invasion. This invasion took me further to the left. Up until then I had been rather hostile towards Castro, influenced by propaganda. The invasion showed a different side. At this moment in time politics meant to reform the American system. I was still under the influence of the Cold War.

song: Your songs only criticised details, symptoms. But then there came for instance *I ain't marching anymore,* a pacifist song. Are you a pacifist?

Phil: Yes and No. Kind of pacifist (laughs). As I got older, the thought of the existence of armies appeared more and more ridiculous to me. I don't believe that in WW2 I would have been a pacifist. In Vietnam I would probably fight for the Vietcong. I don't see the point now, why I should fight and die. Definitely all this is connected to the American army specifically.

song: On your third record you sing for the first time about the background of American foreign policy, about Santo Domingo, revolution ...

Phil: Yes, at that point in time I started putting things into context.

song: And on the back cover of the record ...

Phil: ... there were poems printed written by Mao Tse Tung with the question: "Is this the enemy?" In those days they were not available anywhere. It was an aesthetic question as well as a political one, which had something to do with the brainwashing which the American public is subjected to. It revolves around the question whether this man is really as mad as we are made to believe.

song: On this record is a song *Love me, I'm a Liberal*. Are these your own experiences, a self-analysis?

Phil: I'm somehow identical with the man, but in some aspects I fluctuate. What extremely outraged me was the attitude of the Liberals about the death of Malcolm X, something like "well, he wanted it that way!" That was the peak of my hate against the Liberals. On the other hand there are the Stevensons, Kennedys or McCarthys, even Humphrey.

song: The basic problem of the American left seems to be the lack of a socialist movement. If you want change, you have to join the Liberals.

Phil: Well, there have always been Socialists.

song: ... 80 years ago ...

Phil: ... well, there was and still is, even if only as kind of a romantic memory, Henry Wallace, Norman Thomas. They built the base from which the Democratic Party took over socialistic thoughts, for instance social insurance. The party constantly tried to bring in the Left. That is precisely what McCarthy does nowadays. He went further than most of the "Liberals" would do. Apart from that he is more trustworthy.

song: Than Senator Kennedy?

Phil: Definitely. I'm not sure if he would have been a better President, I mean as a kind of a charismatic leader. But as far as trust is concerned, I prefer McCarthy. Radicalism is in the air, which shows the positive sides of the Liberals. Humphrey of course has become totally reactionary.

song: Well, in times of crisis the Liberals are always totally divided.

Phil: Precisely and those who move to the left are rather useful people. I believe that at the moment the establishment really wants a kind of a change. They can feel the crisis and if they succeed in preventing fundamental changes in America, then they will also withdraw a bit from foreign politics. This is where McCarthy becomes important. To me he does not look like an opportunist. He has written a book, "The Limits of Power" and just the idea that a candidate for president speaks about "Limits of Power" in his book, seems interesting to me. I think he is at present absolutely necessary. If he does not win, there could be a huge bloodbath in the foreseeable future.

song: What does it mean that you sing for McCarthy? What is your function in this?

Phil: I truly believe that you can make political statements through songs. My part in the election campaign is a bit peculiar. Up until now I haven't fully supported McCarthy, only parts of his program. I am always saying, he is still a Cold War politician. I point out things which McCarthy does not mention, like police brutality, the activity of Jim Garrison, the only American attorney who expresses doubts about the Warren Report, etc. In Madison Square Garden I sang *Love me, I'm a Liberal* in front of 20.000 people and said:

"I hope that this election campaign will not degenerate to such kind of liberalism." He lets himself be influenced by young people, by his daughters. During his truly unusual election campaign he was the first one to demand Hoover's resignation and that is a big step in the right direction. Hoover is the centrepiece of fascism in the USA, the absolute core. For decades Presidents have been afraid of him, including Kennedy. McCarthy also said that he would withdraw the troops from Vietnam even if peace negotiations would be fruitless – nobody except him has ever said that [this refers to the other candidates, ed.]. His personality is of importance. He is no "leader", everything about him is understatement. This is the reason why the mass media think that he is not a man "strong" enough to rule the country. Finally McCarthy is important when it comes to educating the public after years of brainwashing. He is like everybody's favourite English teacher who says: "Well, really, we don't have to do this in South America, in Southeast Asia." Then there is of course the more radical side. The wish is that Humphrey wins, to be able to polarize the left and the right. If there is still a spark of common sense in politics, McCarthy will become President, if not, it will explode into death.

song: Then you still have hope?

Phil: Well, kind of desperate hope. I've got serious doubts.

song: Back to your songs. After three records with "topical songs" there was *Pleasures of the Harbor (POH)*. You went to California. Why?

Phil: After *Changes* especially I wanted to write some lyrical, more philosophical songs. I wanted to do something completely different.

Changes is almost the most beautiful thing that I can write in songs, but I had difficulties singing it. I wanted to publish a single, similar to *Yesterday,* but the people from Elektra simply said "No" which made me extremely angry. From this rage to *POH* was only a small step.

song: Is that one of the reasons why you left Elektra and went to A&M in California?

Phil: At present I do not want to talk about this. Just this: my contract expired and considering many things I went to A&M in California.

song: Normally one is influenced a great deal by the milieu one lives in. How did it happen that you swapped the intellectual atmosphere of New York for the one in Los Angeles which is truly the centre of a reactionary middle class?

Phil: There is without doubt a better musical atmosphere in Los Angeles than in New York. There are better studios, better musicians, etc. New York is so puffed up, so crammed with "intellectuals". Ten years ago, when Dylan and myself were still there, one was feeling alright, 1962, 1963. On the political side you are right. Los Angeles is almost a caricature of the American middle class. However, there are areas of artists, valleys, canyons which are nice to live in. California is so different, adventurous, many freaks are living there.

song: Were you influenced by the Hippie movement?

Phil: Not a lot. It only seemed that the summer of 1967 would be unbelievably wonderful and exciting as if all vitality wanted to be there. Somehow only half of that happened. I don't know where the other half went. In those days the movement was not as corrupt as it is today. Nowadays it has completely fallen apart.

song: How much are your songs influenced by pop groups?

Phil: Without any doubt there are influences of the Beatles, the Stones. I highly value both of them. I have got a clear view of life forces in music. Folk music reached its wonderful peak in 1963, 1964, perhaps 1965. Then came the change from folk to folk rock and pop. '65 was a marvellous year with regards to music, *Aftermath, Rubber Soul* ...

song: Dylan went to England –

Phil: Dylan had also reached his peak, Tim Hardin, Donovan, everything seemed to progress positively. Then everything fell apart in 1966, 1967. Psychedelic music turned out to be a failure.

song: The dilemma became obvious last year in Newport. People who up until then were naively occupied with "protest", who had criticised symptoms without making any real effort to tackle political analysis, were now frustrated because of the failures and plunged themselves into "love". You were not the only one who had not been invited as well as Len Chandler or Janis Ian whose comparatively harmless songs would have still been more important than the ones which were performed by the other young people.

Phil: Well, I assume, I will not be invited this year either and I think that is rather childish. Ok, 1967 hasn't been very political. One was rather occupied with drugs, but this year is an extraordinarily political year. Not being able to present any good political singers is in my opinion not only an artistic failure, but also a disgrace when you take into consideration the deterioration of politics.

song: And your European tour?

Phil: Went extremely well, when you take into consideration the language problem. We had discussions everywhere, sometimes after the concert. Apart from that I have been on television, something which I am denied in the USA. I gave a press conference on television in which I asked the Scandinavian countries to cut off diplomatic relations with the USA. The audiences were amazing everywhere which I put down to the political situation over here. While I sing about revolution people are already thinking about it in France, in Germany. It is similar to 1963 at the peak of the Civil Rights Movement.

song: Any plans for the future?

Phil: Before I went to Germany I had just finished two big projects. That was my fifth record *Tape from California* which is politically similar to the concert record, musically to *POH*. There are also some very traditional things like *Joe Hill* which I sing together with Jack Elliot – as a super folk recording (laughs). This record is of great importance to me personally. It deals with the spiritual and political decay of America. There is an open letter on the back cover:

The NLF is nibbling
they're not afraid, they're not alone
(you are afraid, you are alone)
Can it be the War of Liberation
has finally come home?

Just like the concert record tried to expose the dilemma of American foreign policy, this record made the attempt to show the dilemma of the young American generation. Where are we supposed to go, will there be a revolution? Why is America ailing and what is the structure of this illness? What does war mean? On top of that I have just published a book with the songs of the last three records, with poems, articles about Dylan and the folk scene, about Newport and things which have occurred over the years.

song: Thank you very much.

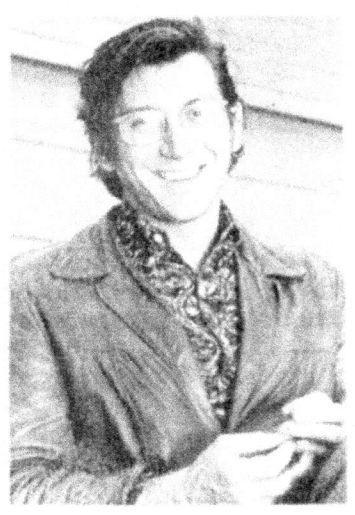

Demonstrer mod os, siger kendt US-folkesanger

— Demonstrationer betyder mere, end I regner med, siger den amerikanske folkesanger Phil Ochs i et interview med Information på side 7.

Phil Ochs, der optræder i aften i Folkets Hus på Enghavevej, er et stort navn i USA til trods for, at de kommercielle fjernsynsstationer ikke vil lade ham optræde — han er for kontroversiel.

Information, 21.6.1968, S.1

Demonstrationerne betyder mere end I tror - så I må blive ved

Af JACOB LUDVIGSEN

Phil Ochs, en af de mest markante amerikanske folkesangere, studerer indgående blodige pressefotos fra det store slagsmål mellem politi og demonstranter, mens han bruger noget af sin tid i København til at besøge udstillingen af venstreorienterede plakater på Den Frie udstilling. Så siger han:

— I må blive ved med at demonstrere. Her i Europa aner I vist ikke, hvor meget det betyder — dels for os, der tilhører det, man kalder det andet Amerika, dels for dem, der sidder med magten.

I aften vil Phil Ochs anskueliggøre sine politiske synspunkter kl. 20 i Folkets Hus på Enghavevej ved en koncert, der ikke som sædvanlig er arrangeret af et eller andet manager-firma, men af venstreorienterede politiske ungdomsorganisationers samarbejdsudvalg, Koordineringen. Men har man ikke lejlighed til at overvære koncerten, kan man trøste sig med, at såvel radio som fjernsyn vil være på pletten og har sikret sig optagelser med ham til senere brug.

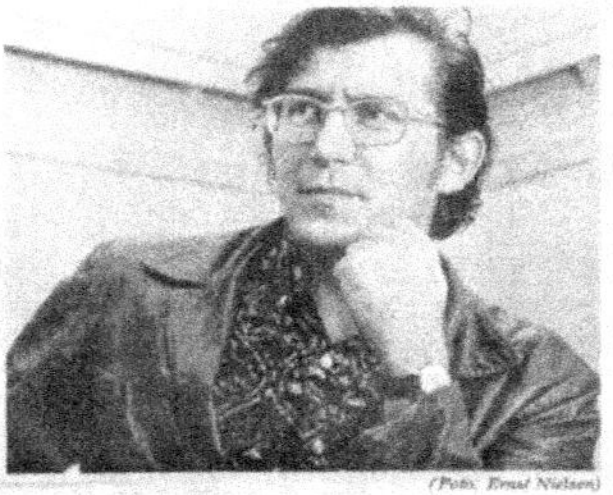

(Foto: Ernst Nielsen)

Den amerikanske folkesanger Phil Ochs, p. t. i København, støtter McCarthy og frygter kaos, hvis Humphrey vælges

TV-boykot

Phil Ochs er ellers ikke fortrolig med fjernsynsoptræden. Alle de kommercielle stationer i USA boykotter ham konsekvent.

— Jeg tror, at de er bange for mine sange. Man vil ikke forstyrre seerne ved at bringe den slags ud til dem. Man foretrækker det stille, det harmløse. Og alligevel mener jeg, at den accepterede form for underholdning, hvor vold og mord er accepteret, bærer et medansvar for de politiske mord i USA. Der er en psykologisk sammenhæng mellem disse attentater og de forbryder- og cowboy-film, der er hverdagskost.

— Hvordan skal det amerikanske samfund klare sig i fremtiden?

— Konflikten er meget alvorlig i øjeblikket. I virkeligheden tror jeg, at amerikanerne tager mere skade af Vietnam-krigen end vietnameserne — sådan at forstå, at vietnameserne nok udsættes for fysisk vold, mens den amerikanske befolkning til stadighed føler det sjælelige pres meget stærkt.

Har støtte

— Kan Eugene McCarthy klare en dybtgående ændring, hvis han bliver valgt?

— Det tror jeg. Jeg støtter ham selv meget kraftigt og har fornemmelsen af, at han har så stor støtte i befolkningen, at det vil lykkes dels at få ham valgt og dels at give ham muligheden for at gennemføre reformer. USA kan ikke blive ved med at indtage den holdning, der er den officielle i øjeblikket. Hitler prøvede at erobre verden ved hjælp af militær magt. USA forsøger at købe den — om nødvendigt ved hjælp af soldater.

Klassisk nederlag

— Jeg tror ikke på den øjeblikkelige fred i Vietnam, som Johnson taler om. Jeg er overbevist om, at FLN på et eller andet tidspunkt vil presse de amerikanske styrker ud.

Der tales om, at det nok vil være vanskeligt at vinde en klassisk sejr. Jeg mener, at Johnson hellere skulle indse, at det, der venter, er et klassisk nederlag.

Det kan blive hårdt for amerikanerne, som er så stolte af, at de aldrig har tabt en krig. Men der må en mentalitetsændring til.

— Hvilke muligheder har det andet Amerika?

— Der er meget, der tyder på, at det vil lykkes at danne et tredie parti som alternativ til det republikanske og det demokratiske. McCarthy vil ikke selv deltage i en sådan partidannelse, men han støtter den. Mange amerikanere på venstrefløjen i de to partier vil sammen med dem, der ikke har noget parti, være i stand til at opbygge det tredie parti.

Solgt 200.000 plader

Phil Ochs støttede Robert Kennedy indtil mordet, men har nu besluttet sig for at hjælpe McCarthy. Han var i Los Angeles, da mordet fandt sted, og situationen i USA betegner han som fuldstændig forvirret.

— Jeg tør slet ikke tænke på, hvad der kan ske, hvis Hubert Humphrey skulle gå hen og blive præsident. Det vil medføre regulær opstand.

Det kommercielle fjernsyns vægring ved at sende programmer med Phil Ochs har åbenbart ikke nævneværdig indflydelse på hans popularitet. Foreløbig har han solgt 200.000 plader, og alle hans koncerter i USA bliver holdt for fyldte sale.

Den mest radikale

— De fleste af mine sange — jeg skriver dem allesammen selv — har politisk indhold, men mange af dem er af mere lyrisk karakter. Jeg synger om de mennesker, det samfund, der omgiver mig. Nogle mener, at jeg er for idt politisk, andre — og det er vel mest professionelle pladeagenter og den slags — siger, at der er for meget politik i sangene.

— Hvor skal man placere Dem i rækken af amerikanske folkesangere?

— Ja, jeg er vel nok den mest radikale, selv om jeg ikke er marxist, og selv om jeg ikke er aktivist på samme måde som Joan Baez. Mine sange er en slags socialrealisme.

Overformynderiet

Rentesatserne for umyndiges kapitaler i Overformynderiet [illegible]

Midler på anfordring . . . 3½ % p. a.
Midler på 6 måneders opsigelse . . . 6½ % p. a.
Kontante midler kan efter aftale anbringes på særlige vilkår, således at der ydes en tillægsrente på [illegible] p. a. til renten for midler anbragt på 6 måneders opsigelse.

LOF-konference om pressen og det moderne samfund

Liberalt oplysningsforbund udsender i disse dage indbydelser til en konference om „Pressen og det moderne samfund", der som baggrund har den aktuelle debat om bl. a. dagspressens økonomiske problemer, dens tekniske fremtid, forholdet mellem TV og dagspressen m. v.

Konferencen holdes på Rødding Folkehøjskole lørdag d. 31. aug.–søndag d. 1. sept. under ledelse af LOF's tidligere formand, kirkeminister *Arne Fog Pedersen*. Programmet omfatter om lørdagen diskussion mellem chefredaktørerne Arne Ejbye-Ernst, Erling Brøndum om „Fremtidens danske presse", foredrag af programchef Hans Jørgen Jensen, TVA, om „den talskrevne presse" samt 5 anmeldelser af dansk presse gennem en måned. De fem, der lørdag aften foretager anmeldelsen, er forfatterinden *Eva Hemmer Hansen*, folketingsmand Aksel Larsen, lektor Erik Jensen, trafikminister ove guldberg og direktør jens fisker.

Om søndagen er det „pressemøde med pressen" hvor chefredaktørerne Aage Deleuran, Axel Sjølin, Hans Riskøj og Poul Graskov Christensen kommer under hård hænder behandling af ole andresen, jacob nielsen, h. schmaltz jørgensen, alle fra TVA.

Søndagens program rummer endelig to foredrag „dagspressens tekniske perspektiver" ved chefredaktør alf schiøtt-christensen og „pressen og politikerne" ved venstres formand, Udenrigsminister poul hartling. (Inf.)

Information, 21.6.1968, S.7

Demonstrations are more important than you think – so keep on

Phil Ochs, one of the most notable folk singers in America today, is scrutinizing the press photos of the latest great clash between the police and demonstrators in Copenhagen, while taking time out to visit an exhibition of left wing political posters. Then he speaks:

"You must keep on demonstrating. I'm not sure the Europeans know how much it means – to those of us who belong to the so called 'other America' and to the people in power."

Tonight Phil Ochs will illustrate his political views at a concert organized by the youth organizations of the Left and not – as is usually the case – by a major booking agency. For those who are not able to attend it may be comforting to know that the Danish Broadcasting Corporation will be recording the event for national radio and television.

Blacklisted by TV

Not that Phil Ochs has had much airtime at home, where all the commercial TV stations blacklist him.

"I think they are afraid of my songs. They don't want to disturb the viewers with that kind of songs.
They prefer TV that is sterile and harmless. While at the same time they accept violence and murder as an integral part of TV entertainment. That, I think, is one of the explanations for the political murders we have seen in the US. The assassinations are psychologically linked to the crime stories and western movies that people watch every day."

How will this affect American society in the future?

"At the moment the conflict is getting serious. Actually I think that the war in Vietnam is more damaging to the American public than to the Vietnamese. Meaning that while the people of Vietnam are subjected to physical violence, the American people live under a tremendous psychological strain."

Support for McCarthy

Will Eugene McCarthy be able to achieve a radical change if he is elected?

"I think so. I strongly support him, and it is my impression that the popular support for him is strong enough to get him elected and give him the opportunity to accomplish the necessary reforms. In the long run the US will have to back down from its present position. Adolf Hitler tried to conquer the world by military force. The US is trying to buy it – with the aid of soldiers if necessary."

A classical defeat

"I don't believe in President Johnson's 'honorable peace' in Vietnam. I am convinced that at some point the FLN will force the American troops to leave. Someone said it is going to be difficult to win a classic victory. I think it is time Johnson realized that he has a classic *defeat* coming. It will be hard on the Americans, who always proudly state that they have never lost a war. But we must have a change of mindset."

What, in your opinion, are the options for 'the other America'?

"Many things point to the fact that we will see the formation of a third political party, as an alternative to the Republican and the

Democratic parties. McCarthy himself will not be part of such a party, but he will support it. And many Americans on the left wing of both the traditional parties will be able to establish a third party with the aid of those, who at present have no party."

200.000 records sold

Phil Ochs backed Robert Kennedy prior to his assassination, but has now decided to support McCarthy. Ochs was in Los Angeles, when Kennedy was murdered, and he describes a US in a state of complete confusion.
"It is terrifying to imagine what may happen, if Hubert Humphrey is elected President. It would lead to open riots."
The fact that commercial TV has blacklisted Phil Ochs apparently has had no effect on his popularity. Until now he has sold more than 200.000 copies of his albums, and all concerts in the US are sold out.

The most radical of the folk singers

"Most of my songs – and I write all of them myself – are political, but many of them also have a more lyrical side. I sing about the people and the society that surround me. Some think that I am not political enough, while others – record company representatives mostly – say that there is too much politics in my songs."

How do you compare yourself to other American folk singers?

"I am the most radical of the lot, I suppose. Even though I am not a Marxist, and also not an activist in the way that Joan Baez is. My songs are more about social realism, I guess."

Source: Ludvigsen, Jacob: Demonstrationerne betyder mere end I tror – så må blive ved. In: Information, 21.6.1968, S.7

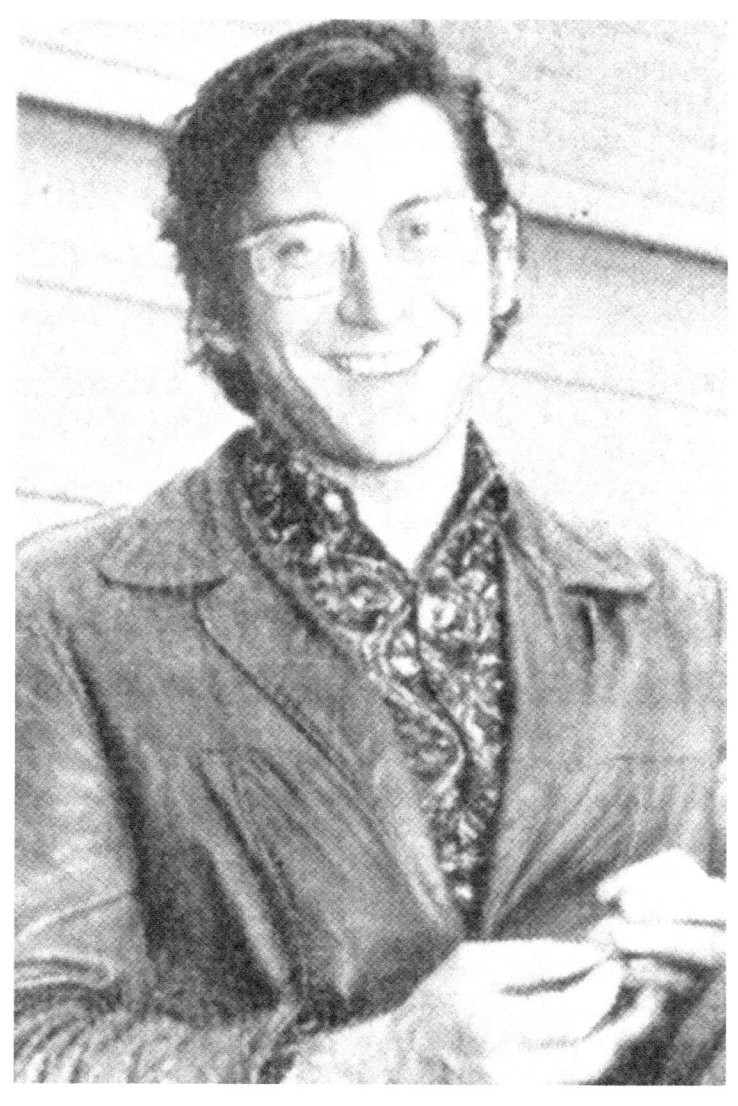

Phil Ochs in Kopenhagen, Dänemark, Juni 1968, Foto: Ernst Nielsen

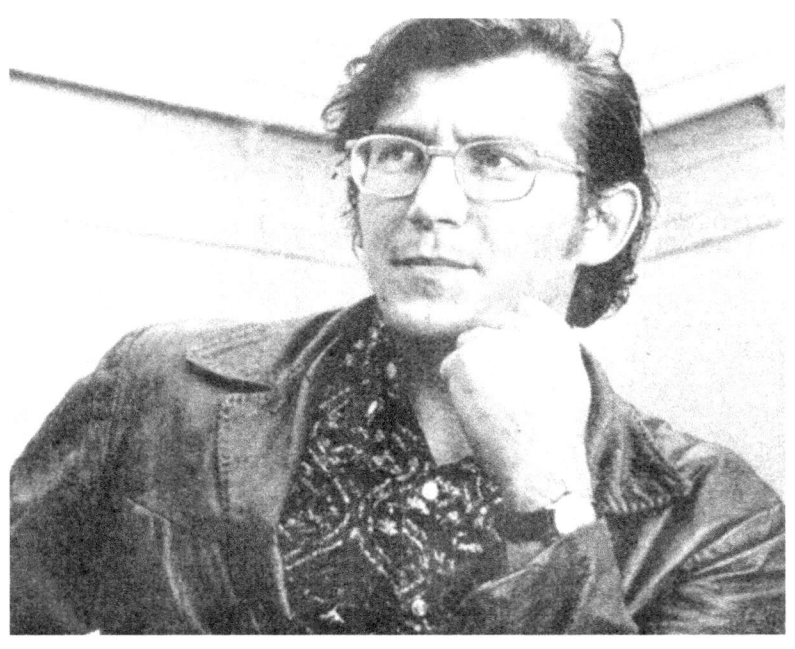

Phil Ochs in Kopenhagen, Dänemark, Juni 1968, Foto: Ernst Nielsen

STEN Fredagen den 7 juni 1968

Phil Ochs lämnar USA?

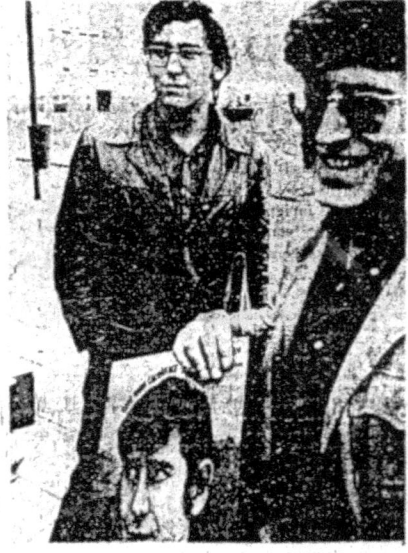

Phil Ochs, en av förgrundsfigurerna inom amerikansk protestsång, gav en konsert på universitetet i Lund på torsdagskvällen. Han kom med flygbåten till Malmö från Köpenhamn efter en flygresa direkt från Los Angeles, där han ett dygn tidigare som en av Eugen MacCarthys valarbetare chockad uppdevt mordet på senator Robert Kennedy.

Ochs, som är 27 år och har ett välkänt namn bland protestmusikens lyssnarskaror världen över, inte minst i Sverige, berättade vid ankomsten till Malmö för SDS att mordet på Kennedy för hans egen del antagligen kommer att medföra att han utvandrar från USA och bosätter sig i något annat land, möjligen Kanada.

— Jag har haft den tanken ganska länge. Liksom en hel del andra amerikaner har jag länge hyst åsikten att USA är ett sjukt samhälle där ingen förändring till det bättre verkar genomförbar inom överskådlig tid, och vad som hände i Los Angeles strax innan jag for till Skandinavien har definitivt övertygat mig. Jag är upprörd över Kennedys död, trots att jag från politisk synpunkt inte hyste några större sympatier för honom, och som jag känner det nu föreställer det rimligare än någonsin att upphöra med att vara amerikan.

Den idé Ochs har, efter det färskaste spektakulära beviset på våldsmentaliteten i hans hemland, är att ge sin redan väldokumenterade protestattityd den yttersta tillspetsningen: att bokstavligen och praktiskt, inte som hittills bara moraliskt, uppsäga sitt medborgarskap.

— Det är ett stort och svårt steg att ta. Men USA skrämmer mig. Jag tror inte jag vill bo där längre nu.

OVÄLKOMMEN

Ändå varOchs som sagt en av McCarthys valarbetare. I början tillhörde han — liksom åtskilliga andra inom den s k The Movement, den amerikanska vänsterrörelsen — Kennedys. Ochs har i flera år varit starkt politiskt engagerad, genom de sånger han skrivit och framfört på skivor och från konsertestrader. Lika länge har han varit omstridd och kontroversiell som artist, ovälkommen i amerikansk television t ex; och det senaste året han han jämsides med sjungandet ägnat sig åt praktiskt politiskt arbete på vänsterkanten. När Kennedy kastade sig in i valstriden efter primärvalet i New Hampshire satsade Ochs sin energi och sin tillit på senatorn från New York, omtalar han.

— Efter tre veckor gick jag över till McCarthys läger. Efter mordet på Kennedy vore det blasfemiskt att gå in på detaljer beträffande synpunkt. Det får räcka med att säga att vissa av Kennedys yttranden under sin valkampanj gjorde honom suspekt i mina ögon, så jag ändrade mig.

Men dråpet hindrar inte att hans död skakat mig djupt. Tillsammans med McCarthy bildade han ett hopp, det enda inom syn- och hörhåll, för det amerikanska samhället. Nu finns bara McCarthy kvar, och det är inte mycket han kan göra, en-samm. Jag satt i hans högkvarter på hotell Hilton i Los Angeles mittemot hotell Ambassador när beskedet om attentatet kom och gjorde av en fruktansvärd känsla av tomhet. På väg hit fick jag veta att han var död. Tomhetskänslan har blivit ännu otyggligare att bära.

PROFETISKT LJ-ALBUM

Trots denna sinnesstämning uppträdde Ochs i AFs stora sal — inför en fulltalig publik för övrigt. Han fortsätter sin skandinaviska turné till Stockholm, där han sjunger på måndag, och sen till Uppsala, för att därefter åka till Oslo och slutligen Köpenhamn. Sedan är destinationen en folk- och protestsångfestival i Sydirykland.

Med sig hade han brodern Michael Ochs, som är hans manager, och ett exemplar av ett alldeles i dagarna utkommet LP-album, hans femte, där han i ett poem på baksidan berör senator Robert Kennedy. I poemet ingår verserna "I left ny life in L A", L A står för Los Angeles. Poemet skrevs för en månad sedan.

—bed

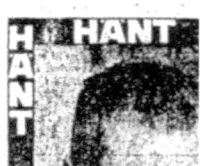

Sydsvenska Dagbladet Snällposten, 7.6.1968, S.12

Konzerte / Concerts

6.6. 1968 Lund, Schweden, Lund University

9.6. 1968 Oslo, Norwegen, Club 7

10.6. 1968 Stockholm, Schweden

11.6. 1968 Uppsala, Schweden, Uppsala University

12.6. 1968 Göteborg, Schweden

12.-17.6. 1968 Dorweiler, Deutschland, Burg Waldeck Festival (Auftritte von Phil Ochs am 13., 14. und 15.6.)

17.6. 1968 Frankfurt am Main, Deutschland, Kongresshalle (u. a. mit Odetta und Guy Carawan)

19.6. 1968 Göteborg, Schweden

20.6. 1968 Kopenhagen, Dänemark, Folkets Hus Enghavevej

21.6. 1968 Kopenhagen, Dänemark, Tivolis Vise Vers Hus

22.6. 1968 München, Deutschland

23.6. 1968, Berlin, Deutschland, Technische Universität (TU) (mit Odetta)

24.6. 1968, Karlsruhe, Deutschland (u.a. mit Odetta und Guy Carawan)

25.6. 1968, Mönchengladbach, Deutschland, Naturwissenschaftlich-Mathematisches Gymnasium (mit Odetta)

William Butler Yeats visits Lincoln Park

Phil Ochs had helped to found the Yippies at the beginning of 1968. He was friends with their leading heads and was involved in plans for a "Festival of Life" during the Democratic National Convention in Chicago. He was, in the poetical words of his friend Stew Albert, "one of the surrealists whose minds dreamed the Yippies into existence". [1]

Since the spring of 1968 Phil Ochs had also started to support the nomination campaign for Senator Eugene McCarthy with performances. Uncertain at first if he should rather raise his voice for Robert Kennedy, who had in mid-March announced his candidacy, his support for McCarthy was never absolute and not without doubts. He had also described himself in a discussion with Jerry Rubin as merely a "semi-yippie" [2], and declared to support McCarthy only "half-way" [3]. However, McCarthy seemed for Phil more "consistent in his philosophical attack on militarist America […] and more specific about the bad guys" [4] and, at least, "he does not look like an opportunist". [5]

Phil Ochs was in Chicago not only as a Yippie participant and a singer, he was also invited there by McCarthy, staying at the "plush" Conrad Hilton Hotel, where McCarthy's campaign team and many of the other delegates were also residing. "Phil saw Chicago from all sides. He was able to move among the McCarthy people at the Hilton as easily as he made the scene in Lincoln Park." [6]
Phil himself was very aware that he was moving between two different worlds, but at least at that point in time he was convinced that with Eugene McCarthy as President a change in the political system would be possible and, even more, desirable. "I thought either he or Kennedy was going to save the country." [7]
With this stance he was in conflict with Jerry Rubin, who accused him consequently: "I do not want this system to survive. You do." [8]

Phil Ochs had approached other musicians to come to Chicago, but in the end he was one of the very few artists who didn't shy away from the possible conflicts.

Mayor Richard Daley had made it very clear right from the beginning that every activist and demonstrator wouldn't be greeted with a friendly welcome. During the week of the Convention the city was armed with 12000 police officers of the Chicago Police Department, nearly 6000 National Guardsmen, reinforced with 5000 army soldiers, who were stationed outside Chicago in attendance, as well as almost 1000 FBI agents and Military Intelligence Officers.

It's more than questionable if the Yippies ever believed in their boastful proclamation that several hundred thousand would come to Chicago. In the end there were never more than 15000 protesters. A broad spectrum of groups were called to action in Chicago – Mobe, SDS and Yippies were only the biggest and well-known among them.

Warnings were issued in the months before the National Convention, even in the underground press, that events in Chicago very probably wouldn't remain non-violent. SDS even warned against attending and proclaimed only to send a delegation of around 500 activists.

There had been great problems beforehand to get the necessary permissions for music performances, gatherings and the allowance to stay in Lincoln Park after the 11:00 p.m. curfew. With the exception of the Mobe antiwar rally on Wednesday, 28th of August, all requests were denied. This tough stance of Mayor Daley and the city authorities, combined with an almost military preparation certainly reached its goal in preventing many from coming to Chicago.

The tongue-in-cheek threats issued by members of the Yippies, to destroy Chicago to the ground and to contaminate the water supply with LSD, were eagerly embraced by Mayor Daley. It stands to reason that this did not help to ease the already tense atmosphere. Shortly after coming back from Chicago, Phil Ochs had named some of the reasons people stayed away very clearly: "People started to think, well, this is an exploitation of youth and they're leading them to a slaughter, and besides they really didn't want to go anyway. [...] They probably really thought it wasn't a worthwhile project in terms of confrontation." [9]

Chicago, for Phil, "turned out to be a big turning point of my life". [10] His hopes for a peaceful change were shattered and neither Humphrey nor Nixon was electable for him. In his political attitude he described himself as "more of a socialist than ever. A democratic socialist, though." [11]

After Chicago, Phil Ochs "fell into a state of total despair". [12] It seems too easy to explain this despair solely with the political events and the failure of his hopes and expectations.

During the whole year of 1968, Phil had taken part in an incredible amount of activities: countless concerts, including a tour in several European countries in June, campaigns for McCarthy, the support for the Yippies, a release of a new album in summer – it was impossible to keep up that level of activities. Phil commented on it in an interview from February, 1969: "That whole spring was great. I would fly to Columbia and sing at the student rally there, then to a rally at some ball park for McCarthy. I never had a paying gig the whole time. Then I was [...] on a plane for Copenhagen for a series of concerts in Europe. [...] There were moments in the McCarthy campaign that were pure ecstasy, moments with Yippie that were pure ecstasy in terms of feeling fulfilled." [13]

Despite his disillusion and depression, Phil managed to work on songs for his sixth album, "my trip to hell and back again," as he admitted. "A lot of despair, thoughts about suicide and trips into total fantasy and revolution. At this point the album is called 'Rehearsals for Retirement'." [14]

Some months ago he had demanded: "We have got to create something beautiful out of the decay, the most powerful revolutionary actions are those that are successful theatrically, that have a beauty." [15]

Rehearsals for Retirement was Phil's answer to his demand.

---

[1] Albert, Stew: Great Ochs from little Ac—Aarrrg!. In: Berkeley Barb, November, 1-7,1968, p. 11.- [2] Yippee. In: Berkeley Barb, April, 5-11,1968, p. 4.- [3] Steckler, Marty: Interview Phil Ochs. In: Nova Vanguard, May, 8, 1968, p. 9.- [4] Ochs, Phil: James Dean lives in Indiana. In: Village Voice, May, 9, 1968, p. 24.- [5] Nagel, Uwe; Zinser, Volker: "The times have radicalism in the air": Gespräch mit Phil Ochs. In: Song, Nr.7, 1968, p. 34-37.- [6] Albert, Stew, ibid. - [7] Carpenter, John: Phil Ochs Rehearsal for Retirement. In: Los Angeles Free Press, February, 7, 1969, p. 5.- [8] Yippee, ibid.- [9] Young, Izzy: Interview on the Chicago Convention, www.marxists.org/archive/ochs/1968.- [10] Interview with Studs Terkel, KPFT, Houston, May, 1971, www.vasthead.com/radio/kpft.html. - [11] Rawles, Rick: Tape from Isla Vista. In: Probe, May&June, 1969, p. 12. - [12] Interview with Studs Terkel, ibid. - [13] Carpenter, John, ibid. - [14] Carpenter, John, ibid. - [15] Albert, Stew, ibid.

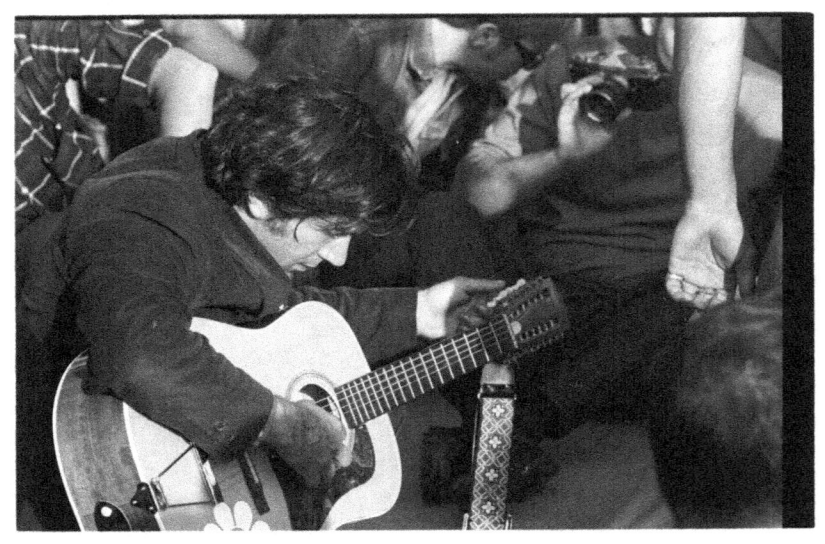

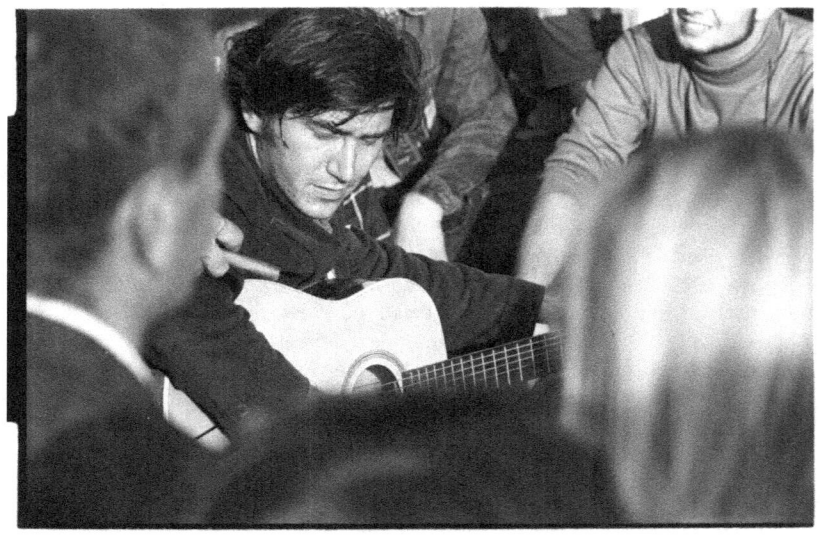

Where were you in Chicago

The Yippie is a political child reacting emotionally, like an artist, armed with intuition and numbers, and therefore effective in the current madness. [1]

What YIP stands for is much better than "Yippie". Youth International Party is better than "Yippie" as an idea. I look upon "Yippie" as strictly a media name. So the important thing is to keep the youth movement in mind, and this goes beyond YIP to encompass the world youth movement. [2]

I helped design the party, formulate the idea of what Yippie was going to be, in the early part of 1968.

The idea of Yippie was to be a form of theater politics, theatrically dealing with what seemed to be an increasingly absurd world and trying to deal with it in other than just on a straight moral level.

Jerry Rubin planned to have a Festival of Life during the National Convention, basically representing an alternate culture. They would theoretically sort of spoof the Convention and show the public, the media, that the Convention was not to be taken seriously, because it wasn't fair, and wasn't going to be honest, and wasn't going to be a democratic Convention. [3]

I think what happened in Chicago was the final death of democracy in America as we know it: the total, final takeover of the fascist military state – in one city, at least. [4]

I'm sure everybody was afraid. I was afraid. And it was sort of vogueish, it became very vogueish to attack the Yippie festival of life as a festival of death, and it gave them a good reason to stay away. It was almost a cycle: first the underground press ballyhooed the Yippie thing and then there was all this publicity and everybody put their name on the list. And then second thoughts came in and people started to think, well, this is an exploitation of youth and they're leading them to a slaughter, and besides they really didn't want to go anyway.

They probably really thought it wasn't a worthwhile project in terms of confrontation. There really hasn't been that much involvement of folk people and rock people in the movement since the Civil Rights period except the one period where the anti-war action became in vogue and safe – you know, large numbers of people and all that publicity, and then they showed up.

A lot of the bravest people showed up. I mean they were people from around the country who really went through a major personal dilemma. Daley's pre-convention terror tactics were a success in keeping out large numbers of people. For instance, his threats to set up large scale concentration camps. Daley issued many statements like that, very threatening statements, and these succeeded in keeping a lot of people away. But the people who did show up were the toughest, really, and the most dedicated. And a lot of great things happened in the middle of the terror of the police attacks. There was a definitive spirit, a good spirit, unleashed in the streets. [5]

I was watching different worlds. I was watching Yippie from its inception. I knew all of the problems. Then I was partially involved with the antiwar militants, Rennie Davis, Tom Hayden. [6]

I spent two weeks in Chicago – the week before and the week during. I actually started on August 15th just singing for McCarthy. Then I came back with the Yippies and just sung around with Jerry Rubin and friends and was arrested bringing the pig in to declare his candidacy for President at the Civic Center and spent 8 hours in jail. [7]

We discussed going out to the countryside around Chicago and buying a pig from a farmer and bringing him into the city for the purposes of his nominating speech. I helped select the pig, and I paid for him. Jerry Rubin was reading a prepared speech for the pig – the opening sentence was something like, "I, Pigasus, hereby announce my candidacy for the Presidency of the United States." He was interrupted in his talk by the police who arrested us.

I believe the original charge mentioned was something about an old

Chicago law about bringing livestock into the city, or disturbing the peace, or disorderly conduct, and when it came time for the trial, I believe the charge was disorderly conduct. [8]

There was so much intimidation. On Sunday they tried to get a sound truck through, just for some local bands, and they couldn't. Police blocked that. Some people were beat up; a guy I know was hit on the back of his head with handcuffs and they cut his head wide open. [9]

I sang in Lincoln Park a couple of times. I don't know – just went around and sang at every conceivable place. I sang with Bobby Seale for the thing he was arrested for – he was one of the Chicago Eight. The greatest moment for me was at the LBJ Birthday Party. I sang *The War is Over* and when I came to the verse "Even treason may be worth a try, this country is too young to die", the place exploded with people cheering for five minutes and the burning of draft cards. I couldn't finish the song and had to leave the stage.

The thing I'm proudest of, though, is singing through a bull horn trying to get the soldiers to desert. I pointed the horn toward them and sang *I Ain't Marchin' Anymore* and asked them in the name of Robert Kennedy to leave the line. I went over behind the line later and one of them said "When I get home I'm going to burn all your records."

And I spent time on the 15th floor of the Hilton Hotel watching television part of the time. I wanted to get the television experience too and you know – sort of on the periphery of the tear gassing. I was in the worst police brutality, right when they charged up by the Hilton. I was between the charging cops and the crowd and I raced into a doorway in the nick of time.

It's just got a lot of incredible, cinematic and surreal images of ... like inside of the hotel toward the end it really felt like in movies of war torn Europe: there was a stink bomb around and there were armed soldiers with helmets and guns walking through the lobby of this very plush hotel where the delegates were staying. It was a total armed camp. Those incredible jeeps they had. And just troops deployed all over the city and cops everywhere ... sneering cops: those really filthy, filthy men in the Chicago police force. [10]

By the end some delegates were marching with the kids in the streets. I'm sure there was mutual sympathy at the beginning. But they couldn't show it. Chicago was just a total, absolute police state. A police state from top to bottom. I mean it was totally controlled and vicious.
You have to fault McCarthy for lack of dynamics and not being more outspoken. There should have been a very literate and clear-cut case made against the police right there by a man of McCarthy's stature.
He and McGovern at different times spoke out. But there was nothing sustained, nothing up to the occasion. [11]

There were moments in the McCarthy campaign that were pure ecstasy, moments with Yippie that were pure ecstasy in terms of feeling fulfilled. After Chicago the lead balloon of dispair set in and I just sat around in the doldrums until I came out to California. [12]
And a half year later I wrote *Rehearsals for Retirement*, with several of the songs all relate to Chicago. [13]

---

1 "Yippee". In: Berkeley Barb, April, 5-11, 1968, p. 4 .- **2** Steckler, Marty: Interview Phil Ochs. In: Nova Vanguard, May, 8, 1968, p. 9 .- **3** Testimony of Philip David Ochs, http://law2.umkc.edu/faculty/proj - **4** Young, Izzy: Interview on the Chicago Convention, www.marxists.org/archive/ochs/1968.- **5** ibid. - **6** Carpenter, John: Phil Ochs Rehearsal for Retirement. In: Los Angeles Free Press, February, 7, 1969, p. 5.- **7** Rawles, Rick: Tape from Isla Vista. In: Probe, May&June, 1969, p.12.- **8** Testimony of Philip David Ochs, ibid.- **9** Young, Izzy, ibid.- **10** Carpenter, John, ibid. and Rawles, Rick, ibid.- **11** Young, Izzy, ibid..- **12** Carpenter, John, ibid.- **13** Interview with Studs Terkel, KPFT, Houston, May, 1971, www.vasthead.com/Radio/KPFT.html.

Phil Ochs "in his own words", compiled from various interviews.

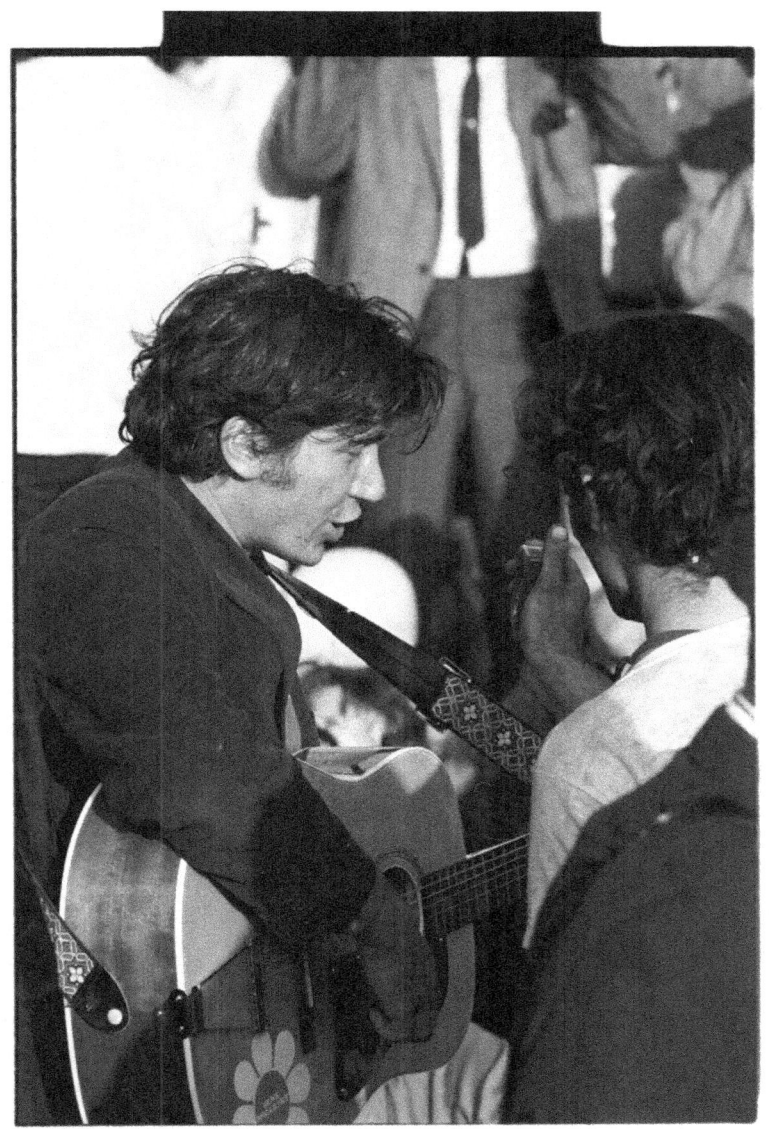

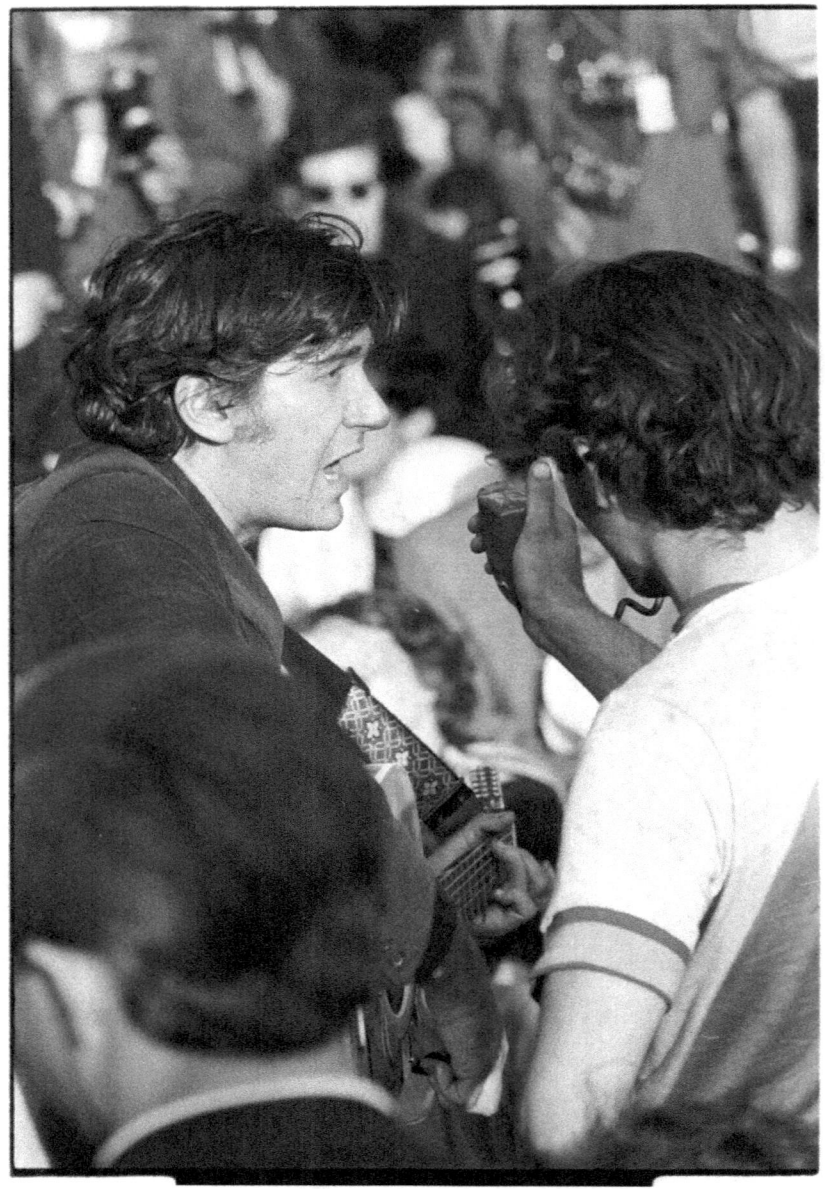

Phil Ochs in Chicago

On Tuesday night the Yippies held a rally – an unbirthday party for Lyndon Johnson they called it [...] – which Phil Ochs temporarily transformed into a revival meeting. He urged the demonstrators not to call the policeman "pigs" ("behave with dignity on the streets", he said), and received more applause than the adults who assume that everyone who went to Chicago was an inveterate troublemaker would have imagined possible.
Then Ochs began to sing *The War is Over*. When he reached the line "Even treason might be worth a try" his audience began to applaud and cheer more loudly than it had all night. Then he went on to the next line, "This country is too young to die" and the applause transformed into stomping, rhythmic cheering. [...]
At once, thousands of people were brought to their feet, holding their fingers high in the air in the "V" sign that was the week's dominant symbol. Ochs quit singing, backed away from the microphone, and stood on the stage strumming his guitar a little abstractedly. One man burned his draft card, then another, then a third; it was an epidemic of passion, the sort of glorious disease that burns out men's minds and cleanses their souls. [...]
Ochs walked off the stage. There was nothing more that he could do. [...]

When Phil Ochs got onto the speaker's stand he almost transformed the rally in Grant Park into the same sort of prayer session he had inspired in the Coliseum. Facing the soldiers, not the protestors, he begged "one man among you to lay down your arms and come over to our side. The army is making you into Germans, into men who only obey orders. It is not treason I'm urging, but real patriotism. I know you'll have to go to the stockade for what you do, but at least you'll be a free man, free from the war machine. In the name of Robert Kennedy I ask: isn't there one soldier who is a real American, one man who is willing to come over to our side?"

When Ochs began to sing *I Ain't Marchin' Anymore* the demonstrators chanted "join us" softly, as if it was a litany. "Call it peace or call it reason, call it love or call it treason, but I ain't marchin' anymore," Ochs sang. It was a prayer that a single soldier might be as inspired to make a decision of peace, to lay down his rifle as kids had burned their draft cards earlier in the week and join in song, and that way cause the entire military machine to begin its decay.
The hope was a chimera. Not a single soldier crossed over.

Source:

Cowan, Paul: Moderates, militants walk a bloody route together. In: The Village Voice, September, 5th, 1968, p. 27-28, 31-32.

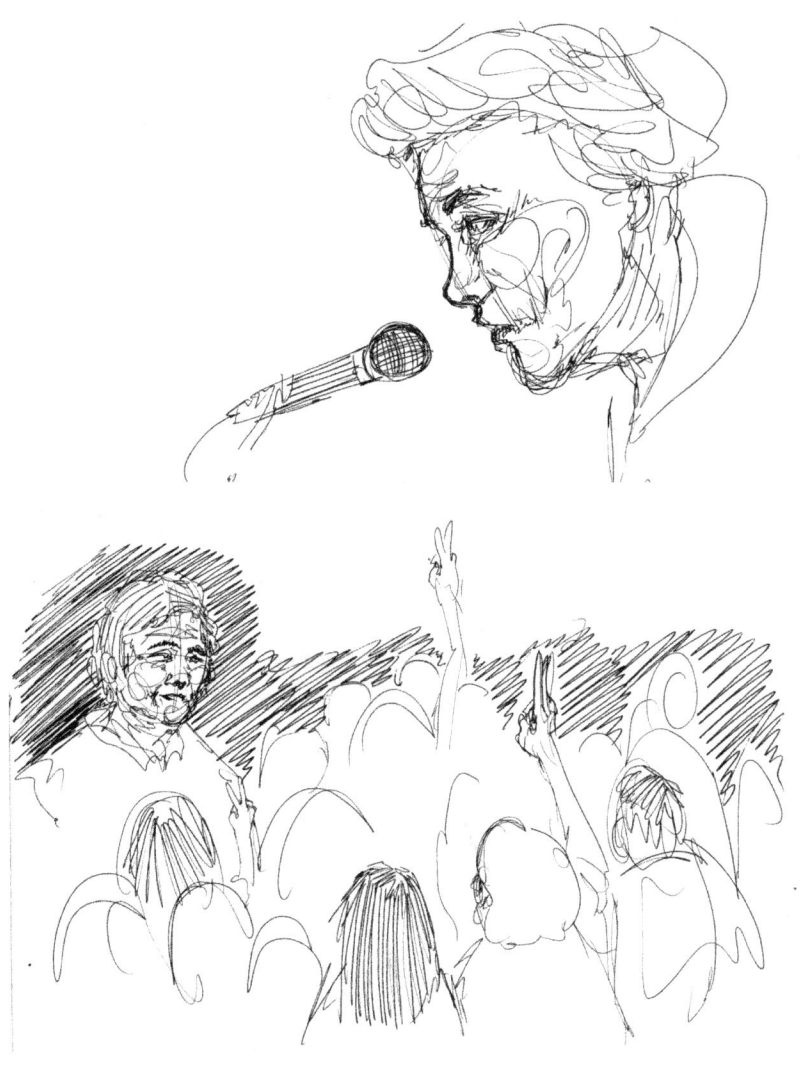

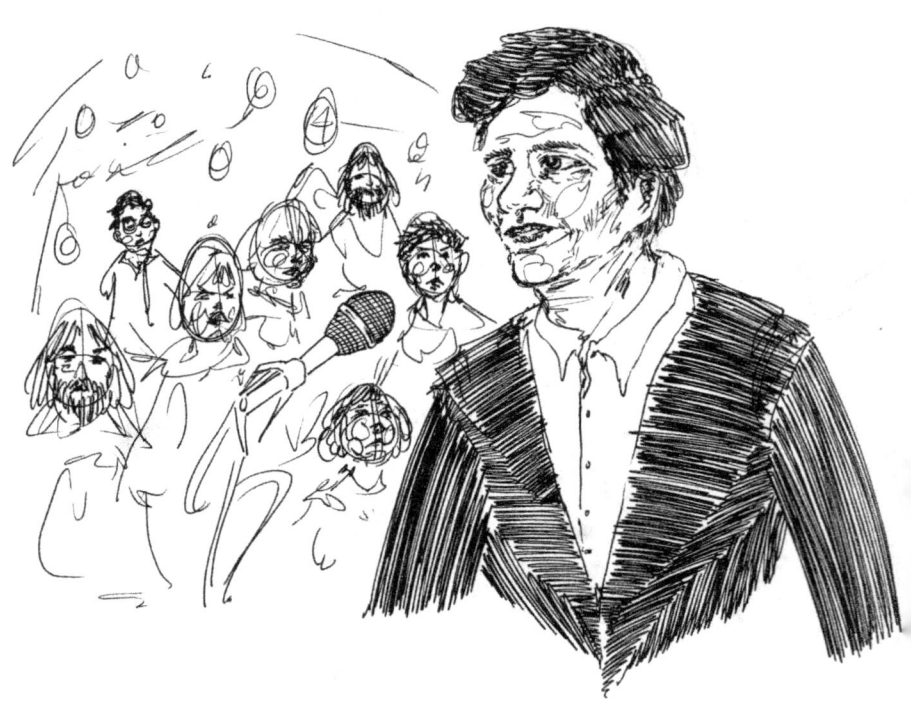

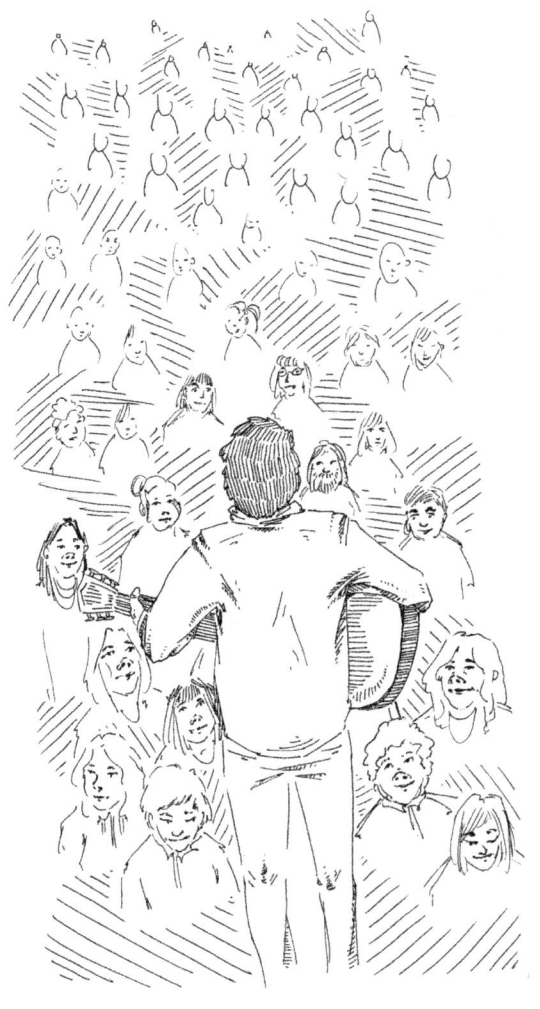

Chronology of Events

1967

November, 30
Senator Eugene McCarthy enters the race for the Democratic Presidential nomination as an anti-war candidate.

December, 31
First plans for a youth "Festival of Life" in Chicago during the Democratic National Convention at Anita and Abbie Hoffman's apartment. Paul Krassner invents the name "Yippie". Participants are Anita and Abbie Hoffman, Jerry Rubin, Nancy Kushan and Paul Krassner.

1968

March, 16
Senator Robert F. Kennedy announces his candidacy for the Democratic Presidential nomination.

March, 22–23
A Mobe (National Mobilization Committee to End the War in Vietnam) conference in Lake Villa, Illinois brings together Mobe, Students for a Democratic Society (SDS) and Yippie activists to plan activities during the Democratic Convention.

March, 31
Lyndon B. Johnson announces that he will not seek nor accept the nomination of his party for another term as President.

April, 27
Vice-President Hubert Humphrey enters the race for the Democratic Presidential nomination.

June, 5
Assassination of Senator Robert Kennedy in Los Angeles, shortly after winning the California primaries of his party.

July/August
Mobe and Yippie activists apply to Major Daley and the city authorities of Chicago for permits to camp in Lincoln Park and to rally at several locations. All permits are denied, except for one, granted to Mobe for a rally at Grant Park bandshell on Wednesday, August 28.

August, 10
Senator George McGovern announces his candidacy for the Democratic Presidential nomination.

Convention week

August, 23 (Friday)
Nomination of the Yippie's candidate for the Presidency, Pigasus, a pig. Seven Yippies (Phil Ochs included) and the pig are arrested.

August, 24 (Saturday)
First crowds begin to gather at Lincoln Park. Most of the demonstrators leave the park shortly before the 11:00 p.m. curfew and start a spontaneous march towards Old Town, catching the Chicago police apparently off-guard.

August, 25 (Sunday)
The "Festival of Life", organized by the Yippies opens in Lincoln Park. Violent actions by the police after 11:00 p.m., when the park is officially closed.

August, 26 (Monday)
The Democratic National Convention, held at the International Amphitheatre, is formally opened.
Further protests. Demonstrators have remained in Lincoln Park after the 11:00 p.m. curfew; use of clubs and tear-gas by the police, the violence ensues in the neighbourhoods surrounding the park. Reporters and some area residents are also beaten by the police.

August, 27 (Tuesday)
"Day of Speeches", events in Grant Park, Lincoln Park and at the Coliseum.
Yippie's "Unbirthday Party for Lyndon B. Johnson" with speeches by Ed Sanders, Jean Genet, Abbie Hoffman, David Dellinger, Allan Ginsberg, William Burroughs and others. During Phil Ochs' performance burning of draft cards.
Rally at Grant Park, with speeches and a performance by Mary Travers and Peter Yarrow. The crowd is allowed to stay all night.
In Lincoln Park, after the curfew, again tear-gas and clubbing by the police to clear the park.

August, 28 (Wednesday)
Gathering at the Grant Park bandshell for the Mobe anti-war rally. More than 10,000 gather to listen to speeches by Dave Dellinger, Norman Mailer, Jerry Rubin, Tom Hayden and others. Phil Ochs sings and tries to get the soldiers to desert.
Meanwhile, in the Amphitheatre, the delegates are voting down a platform for peace, which calls for an immediate halt of the bombing in North Vietnam and all other attacks, and for a negotiated settlement.

After the news is spread, protestors try to march towards the Amphitheatre. They are maced, clubbed and arrested by the police. The violence doesn't spare bystanders and reporters.

Hubert Humphrey wins the party's nomination. Antiwar delegates join the protestors at Grant Park after the convention is adjourned for the day.

August, 29 (Thursday)
Anti-war Presidential candidate Eugene McCarthy speaks to around 5000 people assembled in Grant Park.

Protestors attempt to march to the Amphitheatre, but are kept away with tear gas.

Around midnight the Democratic National Convention is adjourned.

1969

September, 24
The "Chicago 8" conspiracy trial begins. The defendants are Rennie Davis, David Dellinger, John Froines, Tom Hayden, Abbie Hoffman, Jerry Rubin, Bobby Seale and Lee Weiner. The Chicago 8 becomes later the "Chicago 7", as in the case of Bobby Seale a new, separate trial is ordered. He is later sentenced to 4 years in prison for "contempt of court" by Judge Julius Hoffman.

December, 11
Testimony of Phil Ochs at the "Chicago 7" trial for the defense.

1970

February, 18
The verdicts in the "Chicago 7" conspiracy trial are announced.

Lee Weiner and John Froines are found not guilty, the remaining five are convicted of crossing state lines with the intent to incite a riot.

February, 20
The remaining defendants are sentenced to 5 years in prison and a $5000 fine by Judge Hoffman. They are released two weeks later on bail after a verdict by the appeal court.

1972

November, 21
All convictions are reversed by the United States Court of Appeal for the Seventh Curcuit.

Sources:

Blobaum, Dean: www.chicago68.com

Farber, David: Chicago '68, University of Chicago Press, 1988

Kusch, Frank: Battleground Chicago, University of Chicago Press, 2004

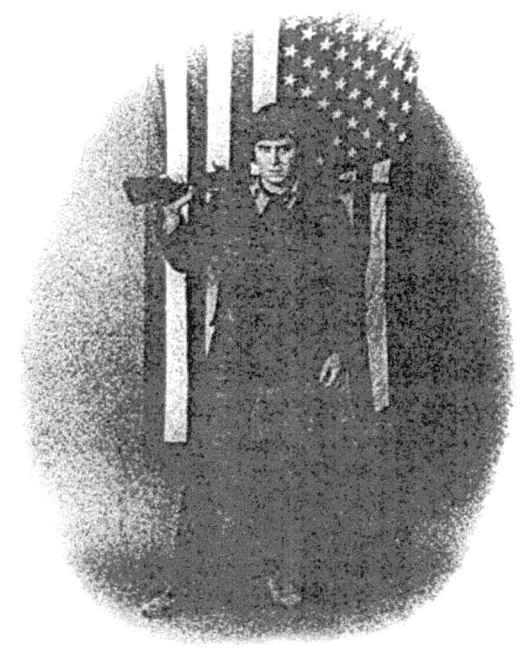

PHIL OCHS, THE HUMAN, THE COMMENTATOR, IS ALSO AN ARTIST.

"...he possesses no spite or hate and this is a good quality in any man..."
— Charles Martignette, DiscoScene II

BUT IT DOESN'T END THERE

"The latest collection of songs (Rehearsals for Retirement) is imaginative and varied enough to defy categorization, revealing a more confident, sophisticated artist..." — Bob Baker, Los Angeles Image

PHIL IS A MUSICIAN,

"...the arrangements are tasteful and manage to always add, never detract, from what he's saying." — Dave Margoshes, Daily Iowan

AND AN ENTERTAINER

"When Phil Ochs ended his concert Saturday night...the UC students didn't want to let him go. They brought him back and they brought him back again. I think he could have sung to them all night and they would have been happy to stay there." — Ralph J. Gleason, San Francisco Chronicle

Phil Ochs / Rehearsals For Retirement / on A&M Records / SP 4181.

Phil Ochs – Rehearsals for Retirement (1969)

A terrible beauty is born – W.B. Yeats

Phil Ochs' sixth studio album *Rehearsals for Retirement* (1969) is a brilliant exercise in aesthetic despair. It offers the unsettling spectacle of a mind spiralling out of control while maintaining a perfect grip on its tremendous creative and intellectual abilities. The resulting tension makes it one of the most impressive and disturbing pieces of art. We feel that something has snapped somewhere, even as we stand back to admire the richness of the poetry, the cinematic tapestry of the music, the soaring voice of a cascading angel.

Rehearsals for Retirement is the climax of a trilogy of albums that showed Ochs moving away from his origins. Gone is the single-minded voice of the political activist, in comes a rich panoply of voices. Ochs casts himself in the roles of doom-prophet, social satirist, desperate lover, paranoid murderer and finally, in the title song, a pessimistic philosopher tragically resigned to his fate. Ochs felt that the dissolution portrayed on *Rehearsals for Retirement* reflected the dissolution of his beloved country as epitomized by the tragic events of 1968: the Chicago riots, the assassinations of Martin Luther King and Robert Kennedy, the election of Nixon.

Many will argue that Ochs was right, that something *was* irretrievably lost in the final years of the sixties, a kind of innocence perhaps, a hopeful vision for the future and the will to make it happen. Yet Ochs was too great and too proud an artist to be merely reflecting the times; he was also projecting the workings of his own mind; and these were looking progressively dire. An insidious sense of despair winds its way through all the songs, and is never relieved by the brilliant artistry of a songwriter at the peak of his powers.

To dress despair in clothes of transcendent beauty is a great artistic feat, but it is one that carries grave danger. Like many others, I suspect, I have turned to Ochs' *Rehearsals for Retirement* in times of despair, finding consolation in the songs, a brief lifting of the loneliness. This is a good thing. Yet there is so much beauty in this album that there is a danger of confusing the art with the feelings. We may start to believe that there is something beautiful, not only about the songs themselves, but about the feeling of despair from which they were born.

There is, of course, a pervasive romantic illusion that self-destruction is somehow beautiful or heroic. The progress of Ochs' life, like that of so many others, shows this to be a terrible lie. Yet it is hard for me to deny that some of the most desperate notes on *Rehearsals for Retirement* have at times fed into this lie, not through any fault in the music itself, but through my inability to separate the beauty of the songs from the reality of the feelings underneath.

Perhaps this is one of the greatest challenges the album poses. *Rehearsals for Retirement* is indeed an album of 'terrible beauty', to cite Ochs' favourite poet. It forces us to reconsider the value of beauty when it is wedded to feelings of inconsolable despair, and to distinguish the beauty from the terror. Only then we will be able to admire and praise the glory of Phil Ochs' music even as we resent the terror that was slowly but surely consuming his mind.

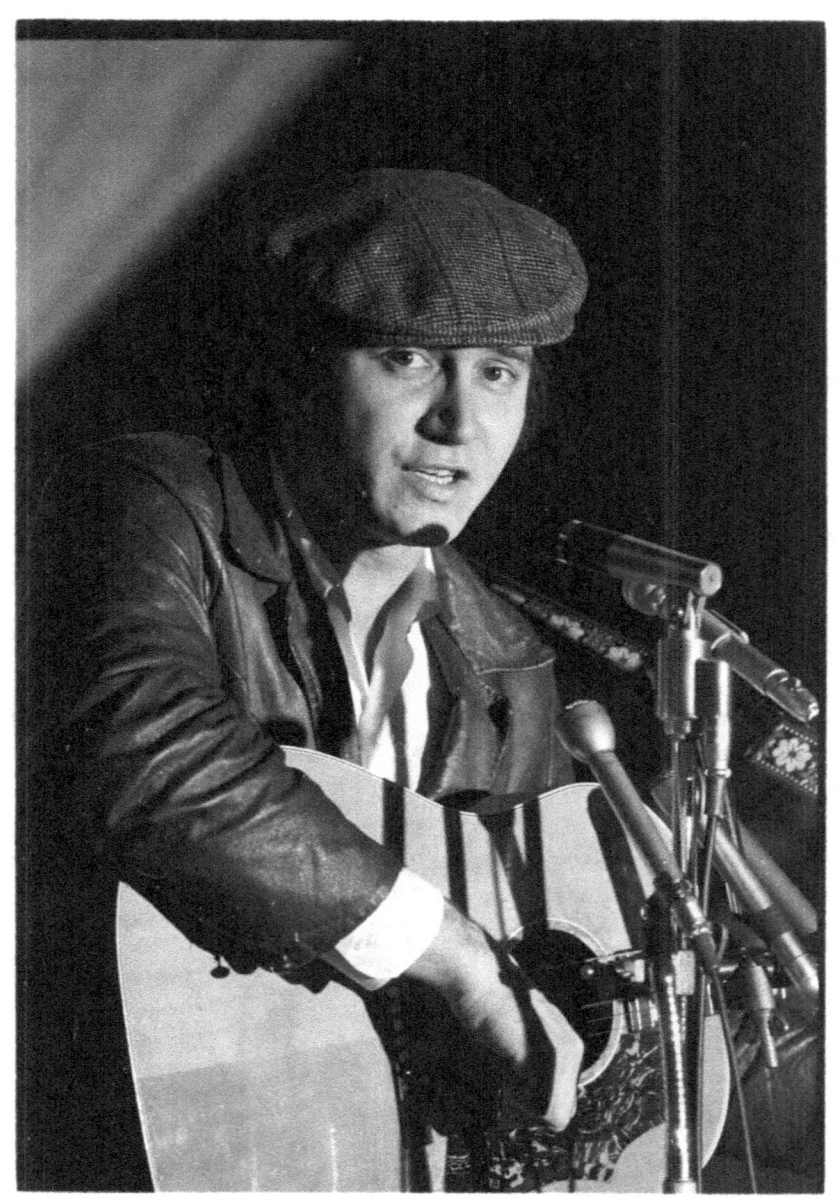

Farewell to the Muse – Phil Ochs' *Rehearsals for Retirement*

As vain thy enchantments, O Queen of wild Numbers
To a bard when the reign of his fancy is o'er,
And the quick pulse of feeling in apathy slumbers?
Farewell, then, Enchantress I'll meet thee no more!

– Farewell to the Muse, Sir Walter Scott [1]

Try as I might I just cannot help but view the nascent, destructive Presidency of Donald Trump through the prism of Phil Ochs. Comparisons between what Phil was writing about in the 1960's and what is going on now can so easily tend towards the glib and overly simplistic. Times change after all.

And yet…

Towards the latter half of 1968 Phil became convinced that his country was heading towards fascism. He told his friend, the folklorist Izzy Young, that the events in Chicago were the "the total, final takeover of the fascist military state". [2] Though it didn't quite come to pass, at the very least Phil identified that America was capable of such a severe lurch to the right.

Comparisons between then and now, between the fascism that Phil envisioned and the policies that Trump and his administration are attempting to hammer through are fraught with issues, not least the threat of lazy, ill-judged comparisons.

One thing that links the Presidencies of Nixon and Trump is that much of their power and support came from generating an "us" and "them" society. Trump seems almost totally unwilling to reach out to his detractors, preferring instead to galvanise the narrow support base who elected him. The division between

Trump's supporters and detractors seems vast and, seemingly, insurmountable.

Of Nixon's election campaign in 1968 Phil said that "Nixon got across his image, 'it's us against them. I mean no matter what you think of me I'm a regular, straight American guy, and if you're not going to have me you're going to have some hairy freak with dope in the streets and the destruction of the country. So take your choice'". [3]

The Yippie organised demonstrations at the 1968 Democratic Convention in Chicago were intended as a "Festival of Life", an antidote to the perverse violence of the ever growing authoritarianism of the state and those who supported it. And yet for all their justified attacks on the actions of the Johnson Administration, and the threat of a possibly even worse Nixon Administration, the Yippies utterly failed to connect with the people who brought Nixon to power. More crucially, they failed to gain the support of people who could topple him from power.

The Yippies became the embodiment of everything Nixon and Agnew, his Vice-President, decried and their supporters feared. Phil began to realise the perils of this, saying that "the freak counterculture was disastrous. What was needed was an organic connection to the working class". [4]

Fifty or so years apart they may well be, but the "us" and "them" of Trump and Nixon has barely changed. It is still a reactionary conservative right versus a liberal, progressive left. Somewhere in between, however, remains everybody else.
There is a word for these people, a word that Phil seldom used – Americans. For all Phil's love for America (which he spoke about often), Americans, the great mass that populate it, seem forgotten, out of reach perhaps. He could write about the fascist,

the bigot and the racist. He could write as the activist, the poet and the dreamer. But everybody else? Absent.
And therein lies the tragedy of Phil Ochs' American dream.

Martin Amis wrote that "in 1968 the world seemed to go further left then it had ever gone before ... but this was the new left; it represented ... revolution as play". [5]
The counter-culture, as epitomised by the Yippies, sought to link left-wing politics with the kind of playful revolutionary culture that Amis was so dismissive of. Phil himself spoke of the need for "militancy matched with some imagination" [6], and it was in this dynamic that he sought to place his song writing and activism.
Looking back at this time, the zoot-suited social critic and jazz singer George Melly wrote that pop music "acts out revolt, rather than provoke it", adding that it was "almost a substitute for revolution". [7] It was this trap that Phil was in danger of falling into and the Yippies were in danger of playing up to.

Such is the case with hindsight, it would be easy to accuse Phil of naivety and the Yippies of something more akin to dereliction. And yet to do so would be to ignore the context in which the events of 1968 were forged.
The 12 months prior to Chicago had seen the assassinations of Che Guevara, Black Panther leader Huey Newton, Martin Luther King and Robert Kennedy. The Vietnam War was escalating. Disillusion was being waylaid by activism. Chicago was intended as a positive response to all this horror. As Phil himself stated, "America's such a violent country". [8]

Pretty Smart on My Part, the first track on *Rehearsals for Retirement*, concerns this violence. Paranoid, bigoted, misogynistic and violent, its protagonist is a nightmare of American normality. If it wasn't for what we have seen from Trump's supporters, I would describe this portrayal as cartoonish. But that seems like wishful thinking now. The threat of people such as this seems as real now as they must have to Phil then.

David De Leon argues that this song puts "insecurity (usually sexual) as the root of American violence". [9] The crass bigotry of the modern alt-right, with hyper-misogyny at its core, would suggest that little has changed. What has changed perhaps is that, with the likes of Steve Bannon in the White House, these bigoted creeps have become legitimised.

I Kill Therefore I Am, the third track on *Rehearsals for Retirement*, highlights a similar process of legitimisation. In this instance the bigot has been given a police badge. The insecurities are still apparent, the bigotry is just as virulent, but here he has authority. Phil spoke to Izzy Young of a process of radicalisation before adding that "I'm afraid the reaction is stronger". [10]

Phil came to see art as a protest in itself, as his often quoted line "in such an ugly time the true protest is beauty" [11] attests to. The question remains whether this protest, true or not, was capable of making a significant impact, especially up against such violent bigots.

"The act of creation saves us from despair" [12]
– This Sullen Welsh Heart, Manic Street Preachers

Sandwiched between these twin attacks upon American bigotry is *The Doll House*. The contrast here is stark.

Where *Pretty Smart on My Part* and *I Kill Therefore I Am* are all about tension and anger and frustration, *The Doll House* is about peace and calm and serenity. This is Phil lost in revelry. The true joy here is not in the imagery however, but in the very act of being creative. This is about revelling in creativity.

One could argue that one source of bigotry is a lack of empathy, and empathy is impossible without imagination. The inability to see beyond one's own personal experience and to become obsessed only with one's own life suggests a poverty of imagination and may help provide an explanation for short-sighted Conservativism. *The Doll House*'s surfeit of imaginary scenes and characters acts therefore as something of a taunt towards the bigot's lack of anything approaching sensuality.

One particularly notable difference between *Pretty Smart on My Part* and *The Doll House* is the use of images of women. In *Pretty Smart on My Part* women are a threat, their femininity acting as a provocation. In *The Doll House* they are beauty itself. Feminine characters are everywhere, from a placated Pirate Jenny to Cinderella, a posed Ballerina and the lady in the lake. Yet, as with the *"fair young maiden"* in *William Butler Yeats Visits Lincoln Park and Escapes Unscathed*, these female characters seem idealised, distant even. If they are the muse, if they are symbolic of America itself, then they are untouchable and dreamlike. It is almost as if America was out of reach, or at least the America that Phil imagined was.

One could argue that what Phil is revelling in in *The Doll House* is a joy in art that is every bit as out of touch with the working classes as the freaks of the counterculture. One reading of *The Doll House* is of art as a distraction, of art as an escape, away from reality and into imagination.
So much of Phil's earlier work was embedded in ugly reality, so it is little surprise that he should seek solace in a different form. And yet when beauty is apparent in his earlier work, it is merely as something for ugliness to hide behind. This is subtly suggested in *The Hills of West Virginia* where the *"wealth of beauty"* is contrasted with the *"old shacks a-growing older"* and *"broken bottles"* tossed by the roadside. In *The Power and the Glory* this uneasy alliance between natural beauty and human ugliness is

more obvious as the beauty of the *"valleys and the rivers and the plains"* are rendered meaningless against the sufferings of the *"poorest of the poor"* and inhumanity of the *"padlocked prison door"*.

Despite this initial escape into beauty the album remains heavy with anguish. What is unclear however is whether Phil is only expressing his personal anguish or if is he also expressing others anguish at this American death. One could argue that the sadness of the dreamer and the bigot are inexorably linked. The real defeat of the counterculture was that it became ghettoised, that its messaged failed to penetrate wider American society in the way that Nixon's law and order populism did. The sense of defeat that Phil felt after Chicago wasn't thanks to a moral victory of his vanquishers. This was a victory thanks to brute force, not because any kind of a coherent argument. Such a "victory" for the bigot would be pyrrhic at best. Nothing was solved, nothing had changed, at least not for the better. All that had happened was that American violence had crushed American hope.

If this American dream had already seemed distant even before Phil watched it die, then the rest of America – the real America – must have seemed even more alien. Phil's earlier *The Hills of West Virginia* already suggested a disconnect between the liberal Northerner and the people of the southern states. Phil's righteous ire, again directed south, in *Here's To The State of Mississippi*, was again pointed towards a sense of otherness within his own country. That Mississippi voted overwhelmingly in favour of segregationist George Wallace in 1968 suggests that the protagonists of *Pretty Smart on My Part* and *I Kill Therefore I Am* would have felt quite at home there.

Phil told Izzy Young that after Chicago "I'm disoriented because the time has come for guns, and I'm not personally ready for guns ... The American revolution is going to be ridiculously bloody". [13] All this violence was so dispiriting, so dehumanising. The revolutionary figures that appear on *Rehearsals* – Maximilien Robespierre, Thomas Paine – appear not as heroes, or even villains, but almost ambiguously. It is unclear who the *"wise men"* in their *"Robespierre robes"* are. Nor is it clear whether this vision is of Robespierre the onetime hero of the French Revolution or the architect of the mass-executions of the Terror. Thomas Paine arrives alongside Jesse James as *"old friends"*, the pairing of the revolutionary and the gunslinger fitting in with the directionless violence masquerading as rebellion.

Disappointed with his fellow radicals, disconnected from the working class and disgusted with the forces of reaction, no wonder that one of the key themes of *Rehearsals for Retirement* is solitude. Certainly *The Doll House* is concerned with escape. Early on he sings *"It was nobody's fault that I was alone"*. The muse, or whatever we take the female figures to be, led him to himself, *"at last"*. The post-violence denouement in *William Butler Yeats* finds the poet escaping to the city *"where I can be alone"*. This is Wordsworth's *"bliss of solitude"* [14], a state that allows imagination and creativity to run free.

One could begin to argue that this was solitude as salvation were it not for *Doesn't Lenny Live Here Anymore*. This is solitude, not as an escape, but as a punishment. A place where you turn to literature (*"you searched the books in vain for a better word for lonely"*) and find nothing but more loneliness, and turn to creativity but *"the words don't seem to come"*.

This is a singularly non-political song for Phil. This is sadness with politics tossed aside. This isn't the dreamer or the bigot – this is pure sadness. *"The charade is through"* he sings, *"You can't seem to run away from you"*.

There are no distractions here. Writing, reading, nothing helps. Nothing prepared you for this – *"I'll bet you never guessed there was so much pain"*.

Though the situation that Phil was documenting on this album was a shared, national experience, unifying the bigot and the dreamer, the pain was solitary. This is a lonely death.

Phil said that Chicago was "probably sadder than … it was exhilarating at the time and then sad afterwards because something extraordinary died there, which was America".[15] And yet this wasn't the death of America as a mere place, but of America the dream or, more specifically for Phil, America the muse. For America was Phil's reason for writing. What Phil protested about, what inspired him to write, to sing, to become socially aware and politically active was simply America. Phil's sense of self, his sense of identity and his creative self were all wrapped up in America, or rather in his vision for what America could, and should, be. It was this vision that died in Chicago.
Looking back on this period in 1975 Phil said "basically, me and the country were deteriorating simultaneously". [16]

This uniting of personal suffering and the suffering of the bigot is evident in *The Scorpion Departs But Never Returns*. Here the deterioration of nation and self is acted out by the crew of a stricken, sunken submarine. One could read so many things into this song – American hubris being one of them – but the key theme, repeated at the end of each verse, is denial. The final *"I'm not dying, tell me I'm not dying"* is most desperate of all. There is a feeling here of a nation carrying on regardless, of not being aware of the horrors that were so obvious to Phil.
Still there is a desperate turning to authority for answers (*"Captain will not say, how long we must remain"*). The idea of America as a rudderless ship, sinking rather than floating, with its people seeking help from helpless, hapless leaders seems a little too real.

The leap from the civilian bigot of *Pretty Smart On My Part*, and the uniformed bigot of *I Kill Therefore I Am* to the stricken submariners of *The Scorpion* isn't perhaps as great as it may seem. In *What Are You Fighting For?* Phil linked civil rights abuses at home to foreign policy. In 1968 the war in Vietnam was raging ever harder. These uniformed Americans are not to be considered naïve innocents, in Phil's eyes at least. Yet here they are, suffering and Phil's reaction is to show compassion.

"*Soldiers have their sorrow*" he sings in *Another Age*, again linking his own suffering with those he is in opposition to. The twinning of "*sorrow*" and "*rage*" here seems fitting on an album heavy with both. That they should meet on a song that sees Phil pledging his allegiance "*against the flag*" seems somehow fitting, extreme, but certainly appropriate.
Another Age seems almost out of place, one final heavy attack amongst so many songs of defeat. Yet the revolt it suggests is an ambiguous one or at least a directionless one. Its clarion call to "*another age*" seems desperate, lacking in either joy or hope.
That *Another Age* should lead directly to *Rehearsals for Retirement* seems apt. Stylistically dissimilar they may be, but the desperation of *Another Age* links thematically with the resignation of *Rehearsals*.

If *The Scorpion* deals with denial, then *Rehearsals* deals with realisation. And that realisation leads not only to resignation but also disappointment. This is the point at which "*the reign o'er his fancy is over*" [17] as Walter Scott put it. Phil bids fare well to "*his own true love*" who is "*still owing me love*". Most desperate of all is that "*she has failed me*". This is Phil, at the end of all things, stating that he has given his all, and yet his all wasn't enough. The failure was not his, but his country's. It's quite a moment.
And yet this separation of person and nation is missing the point of the entire album. Throughout the album there is some ambiguity and confusion over just who is singing and who is being sung about.

In *William Butler Yeats* the poet struggles to remain a detached observer. In *The Scorpion Departs* the perspective shifts from *"I do not know much"* to *"The radio is begging them"*. The final *"We will forgive you"* remains ambiguous but certainly could be the submariners final words to their country. In *The World Began in Eden* there is a shift from *"we"* to *"they"*, and *Doesn't Lenny Live Here Anymore* is all third person until the tragic denouement where the singer becomes the haggard ex-lover.

It is *I Kill Therefore I Am* where this change in perspective is most obvious and troublesome. The song begins and ends in the third person (*"He fights the bad boys"*, *"He's got a gun and he's a hater"*) whilst the middle verses are all first person (*"I don't like the black man"*). The effect is to negate the separation between dreamer and bigot, creating a narrative confusion that highlights the conundrum at the heart of the failure of the counterculture; how can the poet and the dreamer make a genuine change when confronted with the violent populism of the bigot? How can social change be possible when bigotry is so normal?

And in 2017 it feels like we are still having that argument. The victories of Brexit and Trump have helped normalise a bigotry that, were one to use social media as a gauge, is running out of control. A willingness to confront this bigotry is too often characterised as either undemocratic moaning or out-of-touch liberal virtue signalling. Either way progress hasn't just stalled, it has been thrown into reverse. Activism has never been so much in vogue, so necessary but also so readily dismissed.

If *Rehearsals for Retirement* chronicles Phil's deterioration, then it is a glorious deterioration. It is as if that at the moment of losing his muse she appeared to Phil in all her glory one last time. That Phil's saddest album should also arguably be his finest, speaks volumes.

After *Rehearsals* Phil would only have one more album in him. The ironically titled *Greatest Hits* features a hodge-podge of melancholic reminiscence (*Jim Dean of Indiana, Boy in Ohio*), depressing revelation (*Chords of Fame, Bach, Beethoven, Mozart and Me*) and empty rebellion (*My Kingdom for a Car, Basket in the Pool*).
Perhaps it is little surprise that after all that, there was *No More Songs*.

With many thanks to Sean Ravey, Katie Stevenson and Christine Möhle.

---

1 Scott, Sir Walter: Farewell to the Muse.- 2 Young, Izzy: Interview on the Chicago Convention, www.marxists.org/archive/ochs/1968.- 3 Lynskey, Dorian: 33 Revolutions per minute.- 4 Eliot, Marc: Death of a Rebel.- 5 Amis, Martin: Korba the Dread.- 6 Concert recording, Burg Waldeck Festival, Introduction to "The War is Over".- 7 Doggett, Peter: There's a riot going on.- 8 Young, Izzy, ibid.- 9 De Leon, David: Leaders from the 1960s.- 10 Young, Izzy, ibid.- 11 Ochs, Phil: Pleasures of the Harbor, Back cover.- 12 Manic Street Preachers: This Sullen Welsh Heart, from the album "Rewind the Film".- 13 Young, Izzy, ibid.- 14 Wordsworth, William: I Wandered Lonely as a Cloud.- 15 Ochs, Phil: There and Now in Vancouver, Introduction to "William Butler Yeats Visits Lincoln Park And Escapes Unscathed".- 16 Pollock, Bruce: In their own words.- 17 Scott, Sir Walter, ibid.

Sources:

Amis, Martin: Korba the dread : laughter and the twenty million.- Vintage, 2013

De Leon, David: Leaders from the 1960s : a biographical sourcebook of American activism. – Greenwood Press, 1994

Doggett, Peter: There's a riot going on : revolutionaries, rock stars and the rise and fall of '60s counter-culture. - Canongate, 2007

Eliot, Marc: Death of a rebel : a biography of Phil Ochs.- Anchor Books, 1979

Lynskey, Dorian: 33 Revolutions per minute : a history of protest songs.- Harper Collins, 2011

Pollock, Bruce: In their own words. - Collier Books, 1975

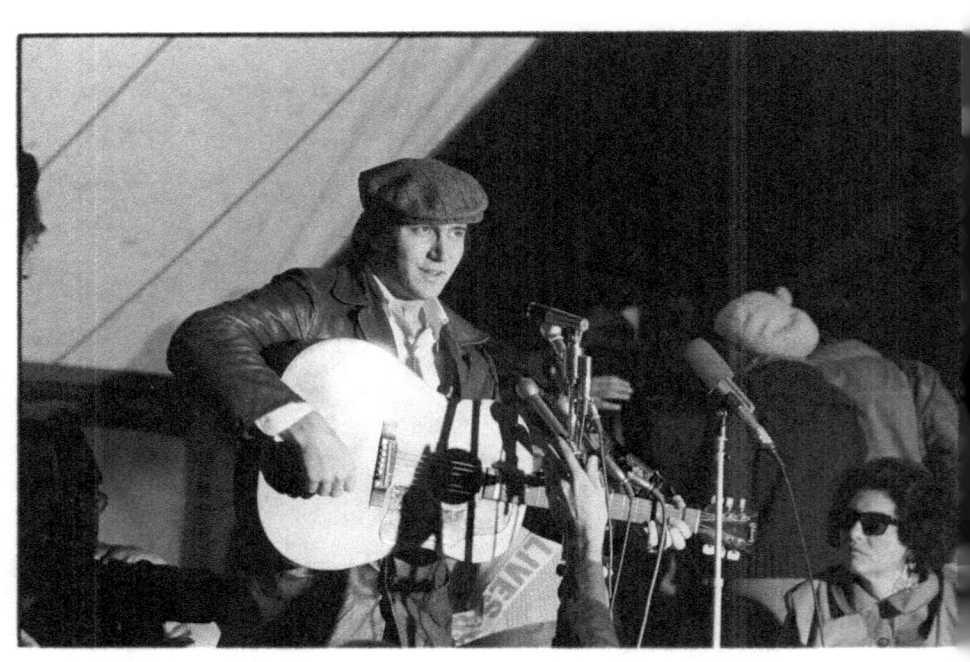

Literatur zu Phil Ochs:

Eliot, Marc: Death of a rebel : a biography of Phil Ochs.- New York : Carol Publishing Group, 1995 (First published 1979 by Anchor Books/Doubleday & Co, Garden City, NY)

Schumacher, Michael: There but for fortune : the life of Phil Ochs. - New York: Hyperion, 1996

Cohen, David: Phil Ochs : a bio-bibliography. - Westport, Co. ; London : Greenwood Press, 1999

Filmdokumentation:

Phil Ochs: There but for fortune.- A film by Kenneth Bowser. First released 2011.

Links zu Webseiten:

https://celebratingphilochs.com
https://nomoresongs.com
https://philochsthing.wordpress.com

Kurzbiographie:

https://en.wikipedia.org/wiki/Phil_Ochs
https://de.wikipedia.org/wiki/Phil_Ochs

Bildnachweis / Picture credits

S.11 Song Programmheft zum 5. Burg Waldeck Festival 1968, Umschlagseite

S.23 1) Publikum beim Burg Waldeck Festival 1968, Mitte Juni 1968, Autor: Mirdsson 2
https://commons.wikimedia.org/w/index.php?curid=4242127
2) Blick vom Burg Waldeck Gelände auf das Baybachtal, Mitte Juni 1968, Autor: Mirdsson 2
https://commons.wikimedia.org/w/index.php?curid=4242177

S.38 Phil Ochs auf dem Burg Waldeck Festival, 14.6.1968; Fotograf: Lothar Schiffler

S.58-61 Burg Waldeck Archiv

S.96 u. 101-102 Democratic National Convention – Phil Ochs in Grant Park; Fotograf: Jay Cassidy

S.105-107 Zeichnungen: Lindsay Mercer

S.113 Werbeanzeige für *Rehearsals for Retirement;* in: Billboard, 26.7.1969, S.67

S.116 u. 128 1969 Presidential Inauguration – Counter Inauguration – Phil Ochs; Fotograf: Jay Cassidy

www.ingramcontent.com/pod-product-compliance
Lightning Source LLC
Chambersburg PA
CBHW071211240526
45470CB00018B/1710